FOUNDATION
BUSINESS

Michael Fardon

OSBORNE

Published by Osborne Books Limited
Unit 1B Everoak Estate
Bromyard Road
Worcester WR2 5HN
Tel 01905 748071
Email books@osbornebooks.co.uk
Website www.osbornebooks.co.uk

Cover design by Hedgehog
Page design by Richard Holt

Printed by the Bath Press, Bath

British Library Cataloguing in Publication Data
A catalogue record for this book is available from the British Library

ISBN 1 872962 14 9

contents

the author

Michael Fardon has worked in international banking and lectured in banking and finance before becoming Managing Editor at Osborne Books. He has written and co-authored a number of financial, business education and Key Skills books and resource packs. He has also been involved in the drafting and editing of GNVQ qualifications for QCA and Edexcel.

acknowledgements

The author would like to thank the following people who have been instrumental in the preparation of this book: Rob Fardon, Hedgehog Design, Richard Holt, Jon Moore, Roger Petheram and Jim Taylor.

Osborne Books is grateful to the following organisations for their assistance and for giving permission, where appropriate, to use original material: Abbey National, Barclays Bank Plc, The Body Shop International Plc, British Broadcasting Corporation, British Franchise Association, Cadburys, Co-operative Bank Plc, Co-operative Retail Services Limited, Co-operative Wholesale Services, Department of Trade and Industry, Malvern Hills Science Park, Marks & Spencer Plc, McDonald's, Nissan Sunderland, One-on-One Fitness Centre, The Post Office, Prontaprint Plc, Robert Hitchins Properties, Tesco Direct, Tesco Plc and Vauxhall Motors Limited.

Lastly Osborne Books would like to thank QCA and the Awarding Bodies for their invaluable help and advice.

teaching notes

the text

Foundation Business has been written to cover the three compulsory Units of the Foundation Business Award:

Unit 1   How a business works

Unit 2   Investigating businesses

Unit 3   Finance in business

Chapter 6 of this book also includes substantial material for Option Unit 5 'Looking after customers'.

The text follows closely the Curriculum 2000 specifications and so is suitable both for the revised vocational award and also the revised Part One.

Individual chapters follow in most cases the topic headings set out in the Unit specifications. These are clearly identified on the first page of each chapter in the box under the chapter title.

tutor pack

A teacher's Tutor Pack has been compiled to accompany this book. It contains essential material such as answers to the financial (Unit 3) Activities, answers to Revision Questions, practice external test papers and photocopiable documents.

If you would like to find out more about this Pack, please contact the Osborne Books Sales Office on 01905 748071.

running order

Foundation Business starts with Unit 2 – business ownership, business activities, location and stakeholders – for a number of reasons. First, the author considers that this approach presents the business world in a wider view and will enable students to gain a sense of perspective before they concentrate on the internal workings of business required by Unit 1. Secondly, the assessment requirement for Unit 2 is for a comparison of two businesses; this again will enable the student to gain a 'macro' view before concentrating on the workings of a single business in Unit 1 which provides a 'micro' view.

There is no reason, of course, why the two Units should not be run in tandem. This would help with the research the students have to carry out; it may well be that the large business chosen for Unit 1 could be the same as the larger business chosen for Unit 2. The text of this book recognises this possibility – there is no suggestion that one Unit has to follow the other.

The Finance in Business unit is placed as the third section in the book because it is more of a discrete entity.

internal assessment and student activities

Foundation Business recommends that students should compile a Portfolio for all Units, including those that are externally assessed.

The Activities in **Foundation Business** (highlighted by the pencil icon) are designed as learning activities to be used inside and outside the classroom.

Answers to the Unit 3 Activities are contained in the **Foundation Business Tutor Pack** which complements this book. If you want further details of this Tutor Pack (which is free with direct bulk orders) please telephone our Sales Office (01905 748071).

external testing and revision

At the time of writing, external tests are the means of assessment for the Finance in Business unit and an optional unit (main award) and for all three compulsory units (Part One).

In order to help students prepare for these external tests and to revise the subject matter, each chapter concludes with a summary and multiple-choice or 'gapped text' questions.

The Tutor Pack which accompanies this book contains practice external tests and gives further guidance on preparation for external testing.

'nesting' Foundation and Intermediate Business

When the Foundation and Intermediate units were first written the intention was that the two levels should 'nest' together. This cosy term means that it should be possible to teach students of both levels in the same class. The units and assessment regimes run parallel. The content is largely the same, but the depth of treatment is different. This book acknowledges this aim and runs parallel with Osborne Books' *Intermediate Business*. The differences between the two books you will find in the Activities – there are simpler, more structured tasks in this book – and in the depth of treatment – there is more subject matter in the higher level *Intermediate Business*.

Key Skills 2000

One of the changes in Curriculum 2000 has been to 'decouple' Key Skills from the mainstream vocational units which constitute the Business Awards. The Key Skills are no longer compulsory, but they do form the basis of the Key Skills Qualification which centres may be offering.

Osborne Books has responded to this by publishing a series of photocopiable packs at all three levels – **Business Key Skills**. These sets of assignments, presented in business scenarios, are ideal for the Key Skills qualification. For further details please access www.osbornebooks.co.uk or contact the Osborne Books Sales Office on 01905 748071.

resources for courses

The need for access to a wide range of resources is mentioned in the 'Student Notes' section which follows. As more and more information becomes available on-line, students should be encouraged to access real businesses and also to make use of the excellent facilities offered by educational websites such as www.bized.ac.uk

feedback

Osborne Books welcomes your feedback on this book. We appreciate both positive and negative comments which originate from teachers and from students. Please let us know by mail, e-mail (books@osbornebooks.co.uk) and telephone (01905 748071) and we will take note of everything you have to say, and will respond.

Michael Fardon

Autumn 2000

student notes

what is a GNVQ?

GNVQ stands for **G**eneral **N**ational **V**ocational **Q**ualification. What is it? A GNVQ is a broadly-based ('General') qualification which is recognised throughout the country – it is 'National'. It can lead to further qualifications or a job. The word 'Vocational' means that it relates to an area of work – in your case the business world. With a Business GNVQ you will be given the knowledge and skills you will need in a business job. A GNVQ means being able to 'do' a job as well as 'knowing' about it. A GNVQ qualification provides skills that employers like; it also enables you to progress to a further qualification.

what is a Unit?

Units are areas of study which make up the course. For the Foundation Award in Business you have to complete and pass six Units:

- **three Compulsory Units** – in which you learn about the different types of business, how they work and how they deal with Finance
- **three Optional Units** – which cover areas such as looking after customers, looking after staff, the environment and personal finance

If you are doing the 'Part One' in Business you only have to do the three compulsory units. All the compulsory units are in this book.

Unit portfolios

Two of the Compulsory Units and two of the Optional Units are assessed through your coursework which is presented in a **Portfolio** – this is a word for the folder containing your work which is known as **Assessment Evidence**. Do not be put off by all the jargon – Assessment Evidence just means the work you have collected together so that you can be graded by your Assessor. The grades you can get are Pass, Merit and Distinction.

Unit external tests

Four of the six Units are assessed by Portfolio (unless you are doing the Part One) and the remaining two – one Compulsory Unit (Finance in business) and one Optional Unit – are assessed by an **External Test** set by your

Awarding Body. These tests are likely to contain simple short answer questions. If you study the chapters in this book and get plenty of practice answering short questions, like the ones at the end of each chapter, you should have no problem passing!

how the chapters can help you

All the chapters in this book begin with an introduction which tells you what the chapter is about and what you will learn.

The chapters finish with a summary and key terms telling you what you should have learnt. Do not skip these sections – they are there to help you.

The chapters also contain Activities for classwork and for investigation.

The chapters also contain Case Studies; when you read these through, try to relate them to situations that you have encountered in businesses that you have investigated, visited on work experience or worked for.

the internet and other resources

In your Foundation Business course you will do a lot of investigation. You will have to find out about a small business and a large business and see how they deal with other businesses and with the public. You will also investigate a larger business in more detail to see how all the different jobs are carried out and how the business manages its finances.

Sometimes it will not always be possible to investigate a business at first hand. You may need to read newspaper articles, magazine articles or textbooks. The best source of information is undoubtedly the internet. You can access business websites direct, you can also look at media sites or educational websites.

Try these sites for examples of businesses:

www.virgin.com   www.cadburyschweppes.com

www.gner.co.uk   www.tesco.co.uk

www.manutd.com   www.halifaxplc.com

www.toysrus.co.uk   www.bbc.co.uk

Try these sites for examples of Government bodies which affect businesses:

www.oft.gov.uk   www.dti.gov.uk

Lastly, for a useful and informative site which contains a wealth of information about a wide range of businesses, try Biz/ed, the educational website:

www.bized.ac.uk

The internet is constantly developing and changing so try browsing around sites. Download and print off financial documents from our own website:

www.osbornebooks.co.uk

Enjoy!

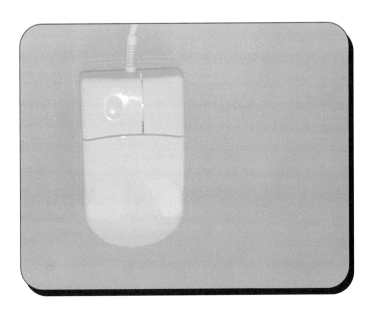

Business ownership

Unit 2: Investigating businesses
Ownership

what this chapter is about

In this chapter we look at the different types of business organisation.

what you will learn from this chapter

● *Being an owner of a business can involve a person in different types of responsibility and involvement in the day-to-day running of the business.*

● *A sole trader is an individual running a business.*

● *A partnership is a group of individuals running a business.*

● *A limited company is a business owned by shareholders:*

  – *if it is a private limited company the public cannot invest in it*

  – *if it is a public limited company the shares can often be bought by the general public*

● *A co-operative is a business owned by its members and run for the benefit of the members.*

● *A franchise is a business with a well-known name (eg McDonalds) operated by an individual in return for a fee.*

● *Public ownership means that the business is owned directly or indirectly by the government and operates nationally (eg the BBC) or on a local basis (local authority businesses such as sports centres).*

now read on . . .

types of business

In this chapter you will be introduced to the different forms of business by Case Studies within Activities – 'snapshots' of people in business, showing the way their businesses are set up, and the way in which they operate.

Look first at the illustration set out below. It gives an idea of the different types of business you will be investigating.

types of business

sole trader

franchise

partnership

public ownership

co-operative

limited company

sole trader

A sole trader is an individual who has set up in business. The sole trader owns, controls and is the business.

The majority of businesses in the UK are sole traders – they include shopkeepers, taxi drivers, decorators, accountants, artists – a very wide range of occupations. As you see they are usually small businesses.

Why do people become sole traders? Because they are their own boss – they own and control the business, and are entitled to all the profit it may make.

But there are financial risks involved. A sole trader will have to provide the money for the business, or raise that money with a bank loan or borrow from friends and family.

In the eyes of the law a sole trader is an individual who has to pay all the debts of the business. If the business fails, the sole trader may have to sell his or her personal belongings or be taken to court and made a bankrupt. Just as a sole trader takes all the profit, he or she takes full responsibility for any losses which the business makes.

Now compare the advantages and disadvantages of being a sole trader ...

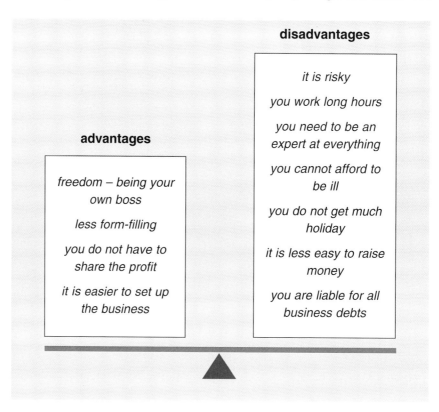

disadvantages

it is risky

you work long hours

you need to be an expert at everything

you cannot afford to be ill

you do not get much holiday

it is less easy to raise money

you are liable for all business debts

advantages

freedom – being your own boss

less form-filling

you do not have to share the profit

it is easier to set up the business

Types of business ownership
Julie Evans – a sole trader

Read the information set out below and write or word-process the answers to the questions on a sheet headed "Types of business – Sole Trader" for your Portfolio.

Julie Evans has recently started work as a self-employed fish seller. She has invested savings of £5,000 into equipment and a van. She has also borrowed £3,000 from the bank to help pay for her van.

Julie has always been keen to be her own boss, and intends to work hard to make a success of the business and make a healthy profit. She does realise, however, that she could lose her possessions if the business fails.

She is confident that she will succeed. She has arranged to sell her fish at local markets and has set up a contract with a fish merchant at Birmingham fish market. She will also sell fish direct from her van in her local area.

1   *What sort of business organisation does Julie run? Name three other trades which are likely to be set up in this way.*

2   *Why do so many people adopt this type of business organisation in the first few years of trading?*

3   *List four advantages of this type of business ownership and four disadvantages.*

4   *Design a business card and a newspaper 'small advert' for Julie Evans. Use a computer package if you can. Make up Julie's address and telephone number.*

partnership

A partnership is a group of individuals working together in business with the aim of making a profit.

Many businesses in the UK are partnerships – they include doctors, dentists and solicitors. Partnerships are owned by all the partners. Partnerships can normally raise more money than sole trader businesses – simply because there are more people to contribute. The day-to-day running of the partnership is normally shared out among the partners – they share control. They also share profits (and losses).

A partnership is easy to set up. Partnerships are often called 'firms' and are regulated in law by the Partnership Act 1890 and in some cases by a written Partnership Agreement. These between them set out:

- the money put in by each partner (the 'capital')
- the money taken out by each partner (the share of profits – or any loss)
- what to do if the partners disagree (it does happen!)

In law a partner can be called upon to pay all the debts of the business. In a partnership – like marriage – you have to be careful whom you chose as a partner. Partnerships can go wrong!

Now compare the advantages and disadvantages of being a partner ...

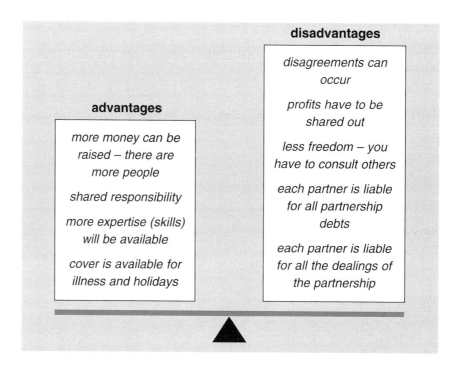

advantages

more money can be raised – there are more people

shared responsibility

more expertise (skills) will be available

cover is available for illness and holidays

disadvantages

disagreements can occur

profits have to be shared out

less freedom – you have to consult others

each partner is liable for all partnership debts

each partner is liable for all the dealings of the partnership

Activity 1.2

Types of business ownership
Smith & Jones – a partnership

Read the information set out below and write or word-process the answers to the questions on a sheet headed "Types of business – Partnership" for your Portfolio.

Smith and Jones are a firm of financial advisers. They offer a wide range of financial advice to businesses and individuals – such as investment advice, tax advice, arranging pensions.

There are two partners; John Smith and Ivor Jones. They operate from a city centre office where they employ a secretary and three assistants. The partners have both contributed the same amount of money (capital), and they share equally the profits of the firm equally. They have both signed a written Partnership Agreement.

1 *List three other types of partnership in your area which provide a service to customers. Write down their names and addresses.*

2 *List three other partnerships in your locality which sell actual products such as clothes or building supplies. Write down their names and addresses.*

3 *List four advantages of this type of business ownership.*

4 *List four disadvantages of this type of business ownership.*

5 *What document would the partners be likely to consult if there was a disagreement between them?*

6 *Smith and Jones want to expand their business and agree to take in a third partner, Amir Patel, who will contribute an equal amount of capital and share equally the profits. What percentage of profit will each partner now receive?*

limited company

A limited company is a business which is owned by shareholders and run by directors.

shareholders

A limited company is set up in a very different way from a sole trader and a partnership business. The owners are the shareholders who have invested money in the company in return for shares and a 'share' of profits in the form of dividends.

directors

The company employs directors (headed by the Managing Director or Chief Executive) to control the management of its business.

who is responsible for company debts?

Shareholders are not responsible for all the company's debts. The most money they can lose is the amount they have invested – this arrangement is known as 'limited liability'.

Look at the diagram below . . .

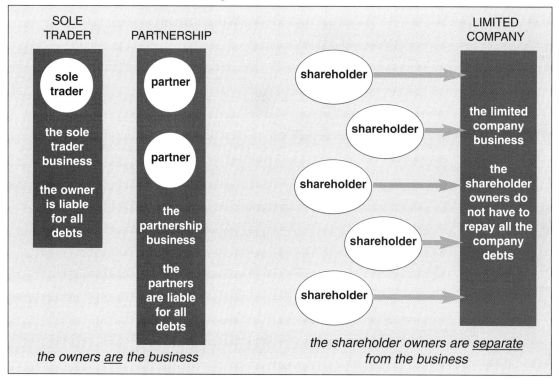

private companies and public companies

If you look at the names of limited companies you will see that they can be followed by the letters – 'Ltd' and 'plc':

R T Designs **Ltd**

J Sainsbury **plc**

The first name is followed by 'Ltd', sometimes spelt out in full as 'Limited' – this is a *private limited company*. The second name is followed by 'plc' – this stands for *public limited company*.

Both private and public limited companies are set up as limited companies. The main difference is one of size, and who can buy the shares.

private limited companies

Private limited companies are generally smaller than public limited companies. Common examples are family businesses such as garages, builders, shops, local coach companies. The shares are not available for sale to the general public and are normally owned by the people who run the company – for example the family members in the case of a family business. These shareholders are often also the directors of the company who own and run the company.

public limited companies

A public limited company (plc) is larger than a private limited company: the share capital (money invested by shareholders) has to be over £50,000. Many plc's have share capital of millions of pounds. A plc can apply to have its shares bought by the general public (although not all do). Lists of public limited companies in which you can buy shares appear in the financial pages of many newspapers and on the internet. If you look through these lists you will see many public limited companies which are household names, eg Eurotunnel, Tesco, Barclays Bank and a number of League football clubs.

remember!

private limited company   -   written as 'limited or 'Ltd'
-   the shares are normally owned by the directors who run the company – which is often a family business

public limited company   -   written as 'plc'
-   the shares can be bought by the public – these are larger 'household name' businesses

Activity 1.3

Types of business ownership

Limited companies

Read through the two Case Studies and write or word-process the answers to the questions on a sheet headed "Limited companies" for your Portfolio.

FOODWORLD LIMITED

Foodworld Limited is a limited company which runs a speciality food store in the town. The business is run by the Oliver family who also own all the shares in the company.

James Oliver is the Managing Director – he deals with most of the food buying and the finance. His wife Anna is the Sales Director and she is in charge of running the shop and organising all the advertising.

Foodworld Limited has just borrowed £50,000 from the bank to expand its premises. The company makes good profits and so will have no problem in repaying the loan. Last year its takings from the shop were £400,000 and the profits were £80,000. The two directors each took a £20,000 dividend out of these profits, leaving £40,000 in the company.

TESCO PLC

Tesco Plc is a leading supermarket in the UK with more than 600 stores. It also has over 180 stores outside the UK and an internet shopping business – Tesco Direct.

Tesco is also a leading seller of organic food and aims to provide value for money for its customers.

Tesco's annual sales figure in 1999 was £18,546 million and its profit for the same year was £965 million.

From this profit the company was able to pay out £277 million in dividends to its shareholders.

1   What form of business is Foodworld Limited?

2   Who owns Foodworld Limited?

3   What do the directors of Foodworld Limited owe the bank for the business loan?

4   Would you be able to buy the shares of Foodworld Limited?

5   How much of the profits of Foodworld Limited did the directors take out as dividends?

6   What form of business is Tesco Plc?

7   Who owns Tesco Plc?

8   What are the sales and profit figures for Tesco and Foodworld? Draw up the figures in the form of a table.

9   Can you buy the shares of Tesco Plc?

10   How much do the shares of Tesco Plc cost? Find out from the newspapers or the financial pages on the internet (try the financial pages of *www.yahoo.co.uk*)

co-operatives

The term 'co-operative' refers to two types of business:

- a retail Co-operative Society – which sell goods and services to the public
- co-operative – a group of people 'clubbing' together to produce goods or to provide a service

We will deal with each of these in turn.

retail Co-operative Societies – the background

Retail Co-operative Societies date back to 1844 when a group of twenty eight Rochdale weavers, suffering from the effects of high food prices and low pay, set up a society to buy food wholesale, ie at the same price as it was sold to the shops. This food was then sold to the members at prices lower than the shop prices, and the profits distributed to the members in what was known as a dividend, the level of which depended on the amount of food they had bought. These self-help co-operatives grew in number during the nineteenth century, but declined in the later twentieth century, largely because of competition from the 'big name' retailers such as Tesco, Sainsbury and Asda.

the Co-op today

A well-known example of a retail co-operative is the Co-operative Wholesale Society (CWS), which took over the operations of Co-operative Retail Services in April 2000. This group of companies is generally known as 'the Co-op'. It operates a wide range of businesses, including 1100 food stores, the UK's largest funeral business, car dealerships, travel services and opticians. It also incorporates the insurance company CIS and the Co-operative Bank.

The Co-operative Wholesale Society also operates a number of on-line services, including on-line banking.

Visit the website www.co-op.co.uk for full details of this group of companies.

who owns the Co-op?

A retail Co-operative Society is owned by its members. You can become a member by filling in a form obtainable from your local Co-op store and buying a share, normally for £1. As a member you have voting rights (one vote per member) and can often obtain discounts at the Society's retail shops and the use of other facilities such as funeral services.

other types of co-operative

The word 'co-operative' also applies to other co-operative businesses. At the time of writing there are around two thousand co-operatives.

trading co-operatives

Groups of individuals, such as farmers, who do not have the resources in terms of capital and time to carry out their own promotion, selling and distribution, may 'club' together to store and distribute their produce. They may also set up co-operative ventures to purchase machinery and equipment.

workers co-operatives

A workers co-operative may often be found where the management of a business is not succeeding and a shut-down is proposed. The 'workers' step in, with the consent of the management, and take over the ownership and running of the business with the aim of 'making a go of it' and at the same time safeguarding their jobs.

co-operatives on the internet

For an up-to-date view of co-operative ventures carry out a UK search on the internet through www.yahoo.co.uk using the word 'co-operative'.

Activity 1.4

Types of business ownership
Co-operatives

Write or word-process the answers to the questions on a sheet headed "Co-operatives" for your Portfolio.

1   *Describe in a couple of sentences the two main types of co-operative.*

2   *Find out where your nearest 'Co-op' is – it may be a shop, it may be a funeral parlour. Try the Yellow Pages for information. Describe what type of products this 'Co-op' sells.*

3   *If you have internet access, log onto a site like www.yahoo.co.uk and do a search on the word 'co-operative'. Describe the activities of five of the businesses which the search reveals.*

franchise

Suppose that you wanted to set up in business on your own like a sole trader, but wanted to use a household name such as McDonalds or Bodyshop. The answer is to set up a **franchise** operation.

A franchise is the situation where an individual – the franchisee – in return for a fee can set up in business using the name, equipment and training provided by a franchisor business such as McDonalds or Bodyshop.

Franchises can be set up as individual shops (eg Benetton), or as services (eg Dyno-rod). Franchises can also be set up within shops – you will often see a Benetton counter, for example, in a department store.

The illustration below shows the way Prontaprint, a well-known name in the 'quick print' business, promotes its business idea to people interested in taking up a franchise.

Prontaprint
■ DIGITAL DESIGN PRINT COPY

REDUCING THE RISK

Starting a new business is daunting. Starting a business which is based upon an established and successful formula is much less so.
A Prontaprint franchise offers the opportunity to enter into an exciting and rewarding market, offering customers a proven high quality product with unparalleled levels of service. As part of an established and highly successful nationwide network of modern business service centres, the risks associated with a typical new business are significantly reduced.

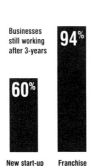

Businesses still working after 3-years

94%

60%

New start-up   **Franchise**

SOURCE: BFA Guide to Franchising

To summarise:

The Print-on-Demand Market
■ Is dynamic and poised for significant UK, European and global growth.
■ Is developing based upon a regional, national and international "distribute and print" model, which will be satisfied by an integrated and high quality Print-on-Demand network. Prontaprint is that network.

Prontaprint
■ Is part of the largest Print-on-Demand network in the world, with a strategic alliance with the US-based Sir Speedy and its affiliates, covering the USA, South America, Australia, South East Asia, Canada and Europe.
■ Offers expert business planning to assist new franchisees achieve business objectives.
■ Provides close links with major clearing banks for investment assistance.

Network Support Centre providing:
■ Intensive induction training.
■ Training in key services; digital design, print, copying, sales and marketing and IT.
■ Structured support from field-based Business Development Managers.
■ New Franchisee Support Team for on-site, hands-on assistance.
■ On-going training and support programme.
■ Expert assistance from technical, IT and purchasing teams.
■ Legal and estates advice.
■ Centralised Prontaprint brand marketing.

advantages of a franchise

- you are going into a business which has been tried and tested in the marketplace
- the business may have a well-known household name
- you are more likely to be able to raise money from a bank for a franchise
- you should receive training and be provided with the necessary equipment

disadvantages of a franchise

- the cost of the fee for going into the franchise
- a proportion of your takings also go to the franchisor (the person you buy the franchise name from)
- you cannot change the business just as you wish – you cannot alter the name or change the method of doing business – if you run a Burger King it has to be the same as all the other Burger Kings

Activity 1.5

Types of business ownership
Franchises

Write or word-process the answers to the questions on a sheet headed "Franchises" for your Portfolio.

1   *List three advantages of setting up a franchise business.*

2   *List three disadvantages of setting up a franchise business.*

3   *Study the table shown below and answer the question that follows.*

franchises – who does what? – some examples	
business	*people running the franchises*
Building services	1080
Catering and hotels	3675
Cleaning services	1775
Direct selling	3995
Parcels and taxis	1520
Quick Printing	600
Retailing	4785
Vehicle services	2035

4   *What types of businesses are franchises, on the whole? Do they manufacture a product or do they provide a service? Why do you think this is the case?*

publicly owned businesses

private and public sectors

Businesses are either:

- private sector businesses or
- public sector businesses

The **private sector** includes businesses which are directly or indirectly owned by private individuals. Most businesses in the UK are in the private sector. They include all the businesses covered so far in this chapter, from sole traders to large companies.

Public sector organisations, on the other hand, are directly or indirectly controlled by the government. They include:

- Public Corporations
- Local Authority enterprises

public corporations

Public Corporations are set up by Act of Parliament, and owned and financed by the State, for example the Post Office, the Bank of England and the BBC.

Public corporations are run by a Board of Management headed by a chairperson appointed by the Government. There used to be more public corporations, but in the 1980s and 1990s a number of them were *privatised*. In other words they were sold off to the public by the government, which turned them into public limited companies, enabling the public to buy their shares.

British Gas, BT and British Airways are examples of privatisations.

public corporations

local authority enterprise

'Local Authority' is a term applied to local governing councils which operate both in the county areas and also in city areas. Local Authorities look after a wide range of services. These include education, environmental health, planning, refuse collection, social services, transport, fire services, libraries and leisure facilities. They finance these from three main sources:

- Central Government grants
- local taxation (the Council Tax)
- income from local authority enterprises (businesses)

Local authority enterprises include a wide variety of businesses, including, for example:

- leisure – swimming pools, sports centres, golf courses
- transport – local bus services
- car parks
- local lotteries

a local authority sports centre

 Activity 1.6

Types of business ownership
Publicly-owned businesses

Write or word-process the answers to the questions on a sheet headed "Publicly-owned businesses" for your Portfolio.

1   *Write down the names of two publicly-owned businesses that operate throughout the UK and state what they do.*

2   *Make a list of local authority enterprises in your area. Try looking at sources such as the 'phone book (under the name of your local authority) or using any website your local authority has set up.*

what have you learnt from this chapter?

● *There are many different types of business organisation, all affecting the owners in different ways.*

● *The sole trader is an individual in business.*

● *The partnership is a group of individuals running a business together.*

● *A limited company is a business owned by shareholders and run by directors. It can be set up as a private limited company or as public limited company.*

● *A private limited company – normally written as 'Ltd' or 'Limited' – is a limited company where the shares are not available to the general public. Private limited companies are often small to medium-sized family businesses.*

● *A public limited company – normally written as 'plc' – is a limited company where the shares can often be bought by the public. Public limited companies include many household names, eg Marks & Spencer.*

● *A co-operative is an enterprise formed by a group of people 'clubbing' together to run a business.*

● *A franchise is an agreement whereby an individual in return for a fee is allowed to trade under a well-known name.*

● *Publicly owned businesses include public corporations such as the BBC and businesses such as sports centres owned by local government.*

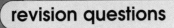

revision questions

Questions 1 - 8

Copy out the following eight statements, having completed each with one of the following words or phrases:

sole trader	**partnership**
plc	**private limited company**
franchise	**local authority**
co-operative	**public corporation**

1   *A person who likes to be his or her own boss is likely to set up business*

as a ....

2   *Shares in a .... can be sold to members of the public.*

3   *Leisure centres, parks and roads are normally the responsibility of the*

....

4   *A family firm that wants to have limited liability for the debts of the*

business should form a ....

5   *A .... is a business which has more than one owner, but each owner is liable for all the debts and dealings of the business.*

6   *A .... is a business in which the owner uses a well-known business name in return for a fee.*

7   *A .... is a business which is owned by the government and operates nationally.*

8   *A .... is a business which is owned and run by its members for their own benefit.*

2 Business activity

what this chapter is about

Businesses carry out a wide range of activities. Some you will be familiar with – for example retail shops, services such as travel agents and manufacturers of products such as clothes and TVs. You will need to think about types of business activity when you are investigating businesses.

what you will learn from this chapter

- *Different businesses carry out a wide range of activities including:*

  - *retailing – small shops, supermarkets, internet stores*
  - *service businesses – banks, gyms, hairdressers*
  - *manufacturing of goods – cars, stereos, biscuits, drinks*
  - *transport – rail companies, airlines, car hire firms*
  - *communications – mobile phone companies*

- *The main difference between these businesses is that some, such as a bank or a gym provide a service. Other businesses – manufacturers – make a product. You will find that there are more service businesses than manufacturers.*

- *Some businesses use natural resources for what they do and need to be near those resources – for example farms need farmland, a sea fishing business needs the sea and a mine needs to be located near coal or iron ore. You may not find these in your area – simply because you may live in an inland town or city. But you are likely to use their products – you may eat fruit and fish and your family may possibly burn coal.*

now read on . . .

how businesses are different

what is a business?

When studying businesses you need to have a clear idea in your mind of what a 'business' is. It could be described as:

an organisation which makes a product or provides a service.

If you think about businesses that you deal with on a daily basis, you will see that they vary a great deal.

Activity 2.1

The range of business activities

Look at the pictures below and on the next two pages and answer the questions on page 33.

1   *Identify the pictures shown here with the following areas of business activity:*

   retailing   manufacturing   transport   financial services

   communications   leisure   using natural resources

Picture 1 is best described as ....

Picture 2 is best described as ....

Picture 3 is best described as ....

Picture 4 is best described as ....

Picture 5 is best described as ....

Picture 6 is best described as ....

Picture 7 is best described as ....

2   *Write a few sentences about each of these businesses, describing what they do.*

industrial sectors

As we have just seen, businesses can be described according to the activities that they carry out. This range of activities can also be seen as a series of stages carried out by what are called 'industrial sectors':

1.   using natural resources

Natural resources are extracted for use in the manufacturing process. Examples of this first stage are mining, farming, market gardening, fishing and forestry. This first stage is known as the 'primary sector'.

2.   manufacturing products

This is the next stage. It involves the processing of raw materials into the manufactured product: fruit into pies or juice, wood into chipboard, metal into cars, and so on. This second stage is known as the 'secondary sector'.

3.   providing services

The third stage involves a business using manufactured items and the skills of its employees to provide a service to the public; examples include shops, fast food, travel and advertising. This third stage is known as the 'tertiary sector'.

Look below at the three stages in the production and sale of a car.

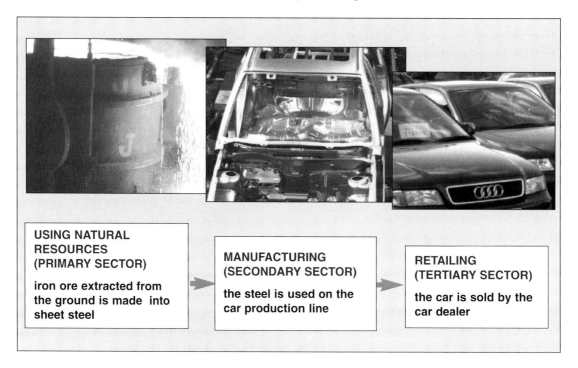

USING NATURAL RESOURCES (PRIMARY SECTOR)

iron ore extracted from the ground is made into sheet steel

MANUFACTURING (SECONDARY SECTOR)

the steel is used on the car production line

RETAILING (TERTIARY SECTOR)

the car is sold by the car dealer

Activity 2.2

industrial sectors

Into which industrial sector would you classify the following businesses? Tick the box you think is correct.

	using natural resources (primary)	manufacturing (secondary)	services (tertiary)
1 a salmon farm			
2 a food supermarket			
3 a car manufacturer			
4 a market garden			
5 a tyre manufacturer			
6 a travel agent			
7 an airline			
8 a restaurant			
9 a catering firm			
10 an oil company			

growing and declining business activities

If you look at the businesses that people deal with in the UK you will see that some types of business activity are in decline while other types are expanding rapidly in number.

Examples of businesses that are in decline are those that deal with natural resources, such as mining. Examples of businesses that are growing in number are retailers and mobile phone and internet providers.

Read through the following press reports and carry out the activity on the next page.

Coal Industry faces extinction

The coal industry continues to shrink as Ellington Colliery, the last deep mine in Northumberland, is due to close. In 1947 there were 1,000 deep mines in operation, employing 1 million workers and producing 186 million tonnes of coal a year. In 1999 there were just 17 pits employing 12,000 miners and producing 36.7 million tonnes. Cheap imports of coal is put down as the main cause of the crisis in the coal industry.

Amazon.co.uk breaks all records

Amazon.co.uk, the UK arm of the highly successful US internet bookshop Amazon.com has now become the third biggest book retailer in the UK, behind W H Smith and Waterstones, after a period of very rapid growth.

Amazon.co.uk despatches its on-line orders from its 500,000 sq feet Milton Keynes distribution centre. Its customers normally receive delivery within 48 hours, sometimes with a substantial discount.

US boss Jeff Bezos says 'Our customers tell us what we want to do next'. This now involves sales of CDs and other merchandise.

Activity 2.2

growing and declining businesses

1   What type of business activity does a coal mine carry out?

2   How many mines were operating in 1947 and how many in 1999?

3   How many workers were employed in mining in 1947 and how many in 1999?

4   Why do you think the number of mines in the UK is on the decline?

5   What type of business activity does Amazon.co.uk carry out?

6   Why do you think Amazon.co.uk is so successful?

7   Can you think of any other businesses that sell over the internet?

8   Why do you think this type of business is increasing in number?

9   The table below shows the value of goods and services produced in the UK by the three industrial sectors from 1979 to 1998.

business activity in the UK
the value of goods and services produced shown as percentages

	1979	1990	1998
	%	%	%
Using natural resources	7	4	3
Manufacturing	37	32	20
Providing a service	56	64	77

Draw a line graph or a multiple bar chart showing the trend over the time period. What does your chart tell you about the different types of business activity?

what have you learnt from this chapter?

- *Different businesses carry out different types of activity.*

- *Some businesses use natural resources for what they do and need to be near those resources – for example farms need farmland, a sea fishing business needs the sea and a mine needs to be located near coal or iron ore. You may not find these in your area – simply because you may live in an inland town or city. You will, however, eat or use the natural resources they provide.*

- *Some businesses – manufacturers – manufacture a product. These businesses include producers of goods such as cars, TVs and food.*

- *Some businesses provide a service. These include shops, gyms and train companies. You will find that there are more service businesses than manufacturers.*

- *Businesses can therefore be divided into three types or 'sectors':*
  1. *the 'primary sector' extracts natural resources*
  2. *the 'secondary sector' manufactures products*
  3. *the 'tertiary sector' provides services*

- *Service businesses are the most common in the UK, and they are increasing in number each year.*

- *Manufacturing businesses and businesses which extract natural resources are becoming less common in the UK.*

revision questions

1   Give three examples of a business which makes use of natural resources.

2   Why are businesses which extract natural resources less common in city areas?

3   Give three examples of manufacturing businesses.

4   Give three examples of service businesses.

5   Which one of the following represents businesses from the primary (natural resources) sector?

   A   farms, fisheries, mines

   B   farms, fisheries, manufacturers

   C   farms, fisheries, banks

   D   farms, fisheries, media services

6   Which one of the following represents businesses from the secondary (manufacturing) sector?

   A   banks, builders, building societies

   B   car manufacturers, TV manufacturers, car garages

   C   mines, financial services, medical services

   D   clockmakers, car manufacturers, paint manufacturers

7   Which one of the following lists businesses which are all from the tertiary (services) sector?

   A   farms, fish and chip shops, frozen food stores

   B   banks, building societies, bookmakers

   C   fitness centres, fish and chip shops, silicon chip manufacturers

   D   taxi firms, train companies, car manufacturers

3 Business location

what this chapter is about

Where a business is located is important to the success of the business. If it is in the wrong place if may fail. There are a number of different reasons which decide where a business is located. You will need to think about these reasons when you investigate different types of business.

what you will learn from this chapter

- *A business is located in a certain place for a variety of different reasons.*

- *A business may need to be near its customers.*

- *A business may need to be near its suppliers.*

- *A business may need to be near its competitors.*

- *A business may need to be in an area where its raw materials are readily available.*

- *A business may need to be in an area which has suitably-skilled people to work for it.*

- *A business may need to be in an area where premises – a factory or an office – cost less.*

- *A business may need to be in an area where it can get financial help from the government.*

- *A business may be in an area because that it is where that type of business has traditionally located in the past.*

now read on . . .

the location of business

choosing a location

What makes a business decide to set up in a certain location? Some of the most important influences are personal factors. In the first place, many businesses are already based in a particular location; history and tradition says that is where they should be. Any expansion or relocation may well be in the same area, because that is where the workforce lives and the commercial contacts have been established. Secondly, the owner of a business may well want to set up in a certain location because he or she happens to like it!

Personal considerations apart, a business will need to ask a number of questions when deciding to set up in a particular location.

do we need to be near to natural resources?

If a business is dependent on natural resources, it is likely to be sited near to the source of the materials it needs. Brick manufacturers, for example, concentrate in areas where suitable clay is to be found. Scotch whisky is highly dependent on the peaty quality of Scottish water and is therefore distilled on site in Scotland. Businesses that bottle mineral water will clearly want to be near the springs.

locating near the source of natural resources

Activity 3.1

Location of business

– being near natural resources

An activity for discussion or for individual work.

Make a list of examples of businesses which are located in a certain area because of the natural resources which are available there.

transport links with customers and suppliers

Some businesses need to be near to the transport system, ie motorways, airports, railway stations. This is important if the business has a large number of sales reps travelling in the UK and overseas. It can then reach its customers more easily.

The transport system is also needed to transport raw materials and finished goods. This may be important for deciding where to locate the business. If a manufacturer relies on the use of heavy and bulky raw materials which are expensive to transport, and the finished product is less bulky and cheaper to transport, the factory will locate nearer to the source of raw materials.

If, on the other hand, the finished product is bulkier than the raw materials, the production plant will be located nearer to the purchaser in order to save transport costs – think of a shipyard building a cruise liner!

Activity 3.2

Location of business

– being near transport links

On the opposite page are extracts from publicity material for a business park in Tewkesbury, Gloucestershire. You want to start a garden tool manufacturing business which needs to distribute its products throughout the UK.

1   Write down what you think are the transport advantages of locating at the Tewkesbury Business Park.

2   Can you think of any other advantages of locating in a country area such as Tewkesbury rather than in an city area like Bristol or Cardiff?

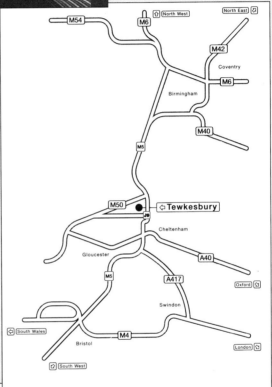

Tewkesbury Business Park is an established business location, strategically located alongside the M5 at Junction 9 giving immediate access to the national motorway network, with both Birmingham and Bristol within an hour's drive. The historic town of Tewkesbury is located immediately to the west and provides excellent amenities and services. In addition, the regional shopping centre of Cheltenham is 9 miles to the South.

Rail links are provided from Ashchurch Parkway (1 mile) Inter-City services are available from both Cheltenham and Gloucester.

reproduced by kind permission of Robert Hitchins Properties

being near the customers?

Some businesses do not need to be 'near' their customers, because their customers are all over the country. Car manufacturers, for example, distribute to dealers throughout the UK and abroad. Their decision of where to locate rests on factors such as the cost of land, the availability of skilled labour and government assistance. Mail order companies, too, sell to a nationwide market, and can locate anywhere within easy reach of the transport system.

Some markets, however, have a very precise geographical location – this is particularly true of service industries. A small business, such as a kiosk that sells sandwiches and drinks must be in the area that it serves.

Activity 3.3

Location of business
– being near your customers

1   Look at the two pictures of businesses shown below.

Why are they located where they are? How important is it that they are near to their customers? Write down the reasons for your answer in both cases.

2   Chose six local businesses and find out why they have chosen their particular location.

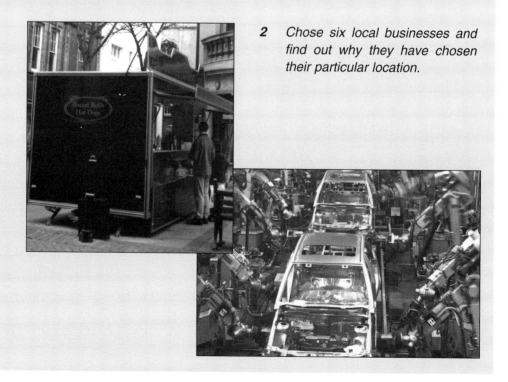

what is the competition doing?

The decision of where to locate a business will also depend on the extent of the competition in the area.

It is often said that the success of a business is based on . . .

"location . . . location . . . location"

If the business is a service business it will need to be seen in the same sort of location as its competitors, for example:

* supermarkets in out-of-town locations
* travel agents and banks in town centres

The reason for this is that people expect to see similar businesses in the same neighbourhood. If a business sets up in an unusual location it may not get as many customers as businesses in the areas in which you expect to see them.

If the business is a manufacturing business the location of its competitors will not be so important – it does not normally deal direct with the public and so often sets up in a business park.

Activity 3.4

Location of business
– being near your competitors

This picture shows three car dealerships in a row. They are situated along a main road on the outskirts of a town.

1   *What reasons have made them choose this type of location?*

2   *Why should they choose to be next to their competitors?*

3   *Find examples of the same types of businesses setting up close to each other in your area – either in a town centre or in a retail park.*

the cost of the wages bill

It is easier to recruit employees in some parts of the country than in others. This may affect the choice of where to set up business. Generally speaking, wages are higher in city areas and in the South East, reflecting the higher costs of living in those areas.

If a business employs many people it may be attracted to areas where labour is cheaper.

Activity 3.5

Location of business
– the cost of paying the wages

Wages per week in the UK regions		
	male	female
	£	£
North East	352	265
North West	365	274
Yorkshire & Humberside	376	277
East Midlands	397	279
West Midlands	367	266
East of England	443	309
London	514	383
South East	458	315
South West	378	267
Wales	334	269
Scotland	382	282
Northern Ireland	307	246

Source: Labour Force Survey

This table shows how much on average male and female full-time employees earn in the different regions of the UK.

1   *Which is the region with the highest wage rate?*

2   *Which is the region with the lowest wage rate?*

3   *If you had the choice, where would you set up a factory employing 1,000 people. Why would you chose that region?*

4   *What do you notice about the wages for women and for men? Can you think of any reasons for this?*

locating where the skills are

The skills of the labour force is another important factor. Certain areas are well-known for particular skills: for example the Cambridge area and the M4 'corridor' for computer technology. Businesses are attracted to certain areas because of the skills that exist there.

In the Case Study below you will see how the technological skills available in Malvern in the West Midlands are used to attract new businesses to the area.

Case Study

Locating where the skills are
Malvern Hills Science Park

The Malvern Hills Science Park is a purpose-built complex suitable for office and laboratory use.

The skills available locally are those developed in the government-run DERA (Defence Evaluation and Research Agency).

DERA has had a hand in innovations such as radar, liquid crystal flat panel displays and the technology used in thermal imaging cameras.

Some of the world's most technically adventurous people are making their way to Malvern. Amongst them are companies, large and small, from Japan and America, from Taiwan and from Continental Europe. Some are existing sector leaders and some are small ambitious newcomers. Many are companies working in leading edge research and others are seeking solutions to everyday technical problems. All believe that the key to their future prosperity is to be found there. *Why?*

An amazing range of technologies has been developed over many years within the Defence Evaluation and Research Agency (DERA) for military use. The British Government is keen that this expertise should, where strategically acceptable, be made accessible to companies able to develop productive relationships with DERA. They want to enhance Great Britain's technological strengths and to develop centres of excellence that will be the envy of the world.

You and your staff can now interact creatively with free thinking specialists in your own field. They will bring fresh minds and access to undreamed of technologies to address your problems.

The Malvern Hills Science Park is located immediately adjacent to the DERA site in Malvern. Situated in an area of outstanding natural beauty at the foot of the Malvern Hills, the Science Park is at the heart of a region of emerging technology-based companies.

It has excellent road and rail links to the Midlands, London, Wales and the North and is conveniently situated for Birmingham International and London Heathrow airports.

By Road:

M5 and M50	20 minutes
London Heathrow	2 hours
Birmingham International Airport	1 hour 15 minutes
Oxford	1 hour 20 minutes

By Rail:

Great Malvern - London (direct)	2 hours 15 minutes
Great Malvern - Birmingham New Street	1 hour

Source: Malvern Hills Science Park

Activity 3.6

Locating where the skills are Malvern Hills Science Park

1 *What special skills are available in the Malvern area?*

2 *What type of technology has been developed in Malvern?*

3 *Where are the new businesses coming from?*

4 *What other reasons might attract businesses to the Malvern area?*

help from the Government

The UK Government provides financial help – Regional Selective Assistance – to businesses setting up in areas which have low levels of earnings and high unemployment.

This assistance – grants, cheap rents, free and subsidised advice – is administered through the Department of Trade and Industry, normally referred to as 'the DTI'.

Businesses setting up for the first time, or moving, receive great benefits from setting up in these 'Assisted Areas'.

The areas which receive this Government assistance are shown in the map below.

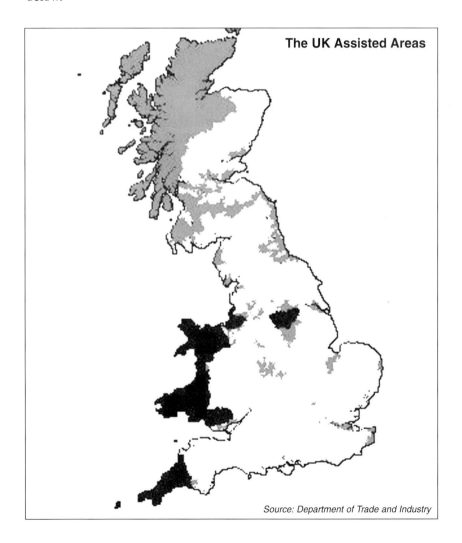

The UK Assisted Areas

Source: Department of Trade and Industry

what have you learnt from this chapter?

● *A business will set up and operate from a particular location for a number of different reasons.*

● *Some businesses choose a location for personal, traditional and historical reasons, saying things like – 'because we have always been based here' or 'this type of business has always been found in this area'.*

● *Some businesses which use natural resources – for example water, wood, oil – find it more convenient and cheaper to operate from the places where the resources are found.*

● *Being near to good transport links is an important factor for businesses that*

   – need to deliver goods to their customers

   – want to be near to their suppliers

   – rely on good transport links for their sales force

● *Many businesses – particularly service businesses such as shops and hairdressers – need to be located near to their customers.*

● *Businesses often also need to be near their competitors. This is mainly so that their customers can compare their products with those of their competitors.*

● *Businesses such as manufacturers that employ a large number of employees often prefer to locate where the wage rates are lower. This saves them money.*

● *Businesses which need financial help – eg for premises – can set up in 'Assisted Areas' which qualify for government grants and advice services.*

revision questions

Complete each of the sentences below (Questions 1 to 3) using one of the following phrases:

lower cost of labour   skilled workforce   Government grant

1   *A business which develops new computer technology is most likely to*

    locate in an area which has a ....
    trained in computer technology.

2   *A business which is setting up a factory employing 2,000 staff will be able to save on its labour costs by setting up in an area with a*

    ...

3   *A business which needs to build a new factory could obtain a*

    .. by setting up in an Assisted Area.

4   *The need to locate a business near the supply of natural resources is likely to be most important for (choose one answer from A,B,C & D)*
    A   *a car manufacturer*
    B   *a holiday company*
    C   *a mineral water bottling plant*
    D   *an insurance company*

5   *The need to locate a business near the UK motorway network is likely to be most important for (choose one answer from A,B,C & D)*
    A   *a company that manufactures cars*
    B   *a company that sells holidays*
    C   *a manufacturer that distributes its own products*
    D   *a farming co-operative*

6   *The need to locate a business near its customers is likely to be most important for (choose one answer from A,B,C & D)*
    A   *a shoe shop*
    B   *a manufacturer*
    C   *a mail order company*
    D   *a farmer*

4

Stakeholders

what this chapter is about

Stakeholders are people who have an interest – a 'stake' – of some sort in a business. They can work in the business – for example employees and managers. They can be completely separate from the business – for example customers and the local community. It is important that the management that runs a business takes account of the needs and opinions of stakeholders.

what you will learn from this chapter

- *Different types of business have different types of stakeholder – generally speaking the larger the business the greater the number of stakeholders.*

- *Customers are very important stakeholders – if the business keeps its customers happy it will normally maintain a good level of sales and be successful.*

- *Employees and managers work inside the business. A successful business will take account of their views and make sure they are well trained to ensure the business is well run.*

- *The owners of a business – for example the shareholders of a limited company – look for a return on their money.*

- *The local community and environmental pressure groups also have an interest in business – they want the community to benefit from businesses and they need to know that businesses are caring for the environment.*

- *The government has an interest as a stakeholder. It creates laws for the regulation of businesses and it collects taxes from businesses to pay for government spending on areas such as health and education.*

now read on . . .

stakeholders

what are stakeholders?

Stakeholders are people who have an interest – a 'stake' – in the business. It matters to them what the business does. These people may own shares in the business, or they may be affected by the activities of the business. They may work in the business (internal stakeholders) or they may be outsiders (external stakeholders).

Stakeholders include:

- customers
- employees and managers who work in the business
- shareholders
- the local community
- the government

We will look at how each of these types of stakeholder has an interest in the business and why they are important to the business.

Look at the diagram below and then read on . . .

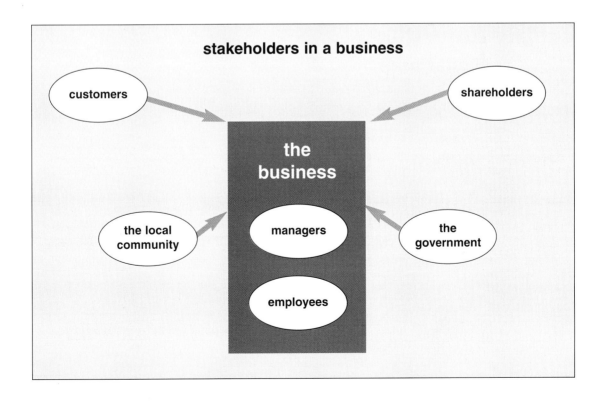

taking notice of stakeholders

Stakeholders and their views are important to a business. If a business ignores the needs of its customers by having unsocial opening hours, or if it pollutes the atmosphere it will find that public opinion is likely to turn against it. It will lose custom and it will then lose profits.

customers

Many businesses are nowadays 'customer-focused'. This means that they aim to keep their customers happy by looking after them, listening to their views and meeting their needs. With businesses in such keen competition, a customer ignored is a customer that is lost.

If customers' views are not taken into account, the results can be serious. Customers are often represented by pressure groups such as Greenpeace, which campaigns on environmental issues.

Another result of customer pressure being exerted are on supermarkets is the increasing sales of organic food and the withdrawal of some genetically modified foods.

Activity 4.1

Stakeholders
– customers

Visit your local supermarket or find out about supermarkets from people who do the shopping for your household.

1   *Make a list of the facilities the supermarket offers to its shoppers – for example hot food and drink, petrol, bottle banks.*

2   *What stakeholders benefit from these facilities?*

3   *Why should the supermarket go to the expense of providing these facilities?*

4   *What do you think would happen if the supermarket did not provide these facilities?*

5   *Can you think of any other facilities a supermarket might usefully offer?*

employees and managers

People who work in a business and their managers are also stakeholders.

employees as stakeholders

Employees are stakeholders in a business because they have an interest in a comfortable working environment, good rates of pay, training and promotion prospects. If the owners of a business neglect employee training, welfare and pay levels in the interests of profits, it is likely to lose them money in the long run.

Businesses are also involving employees more and more in decision-making; some have set up 'team-working' as a method of working. This is where every employee has a 'say' in the way the business operates.

managers as stakeholders

Managers are employees who have a higher degree of control and decision-making than the more junior employee. They are stakeholders because the success of the business will bring them satisfaction and, in some case, money bonuses related to their success rate.

Activity 4.2

Stakeholders

– employees and managers

Craig is a manager in a cosmetics company and Sam is a trainee sales representative.

1   *What interests in the business does Craig have as a stakeholder?*

2   *What interests in the business does Sam have as a stakeholder?*

shareholders

A shareholder is a person who has invested money in a limited company. The money is invested in the form of 'shares'.

A shareholder will receive a share of the profit of the limited company business in the form of a payment known as a 'dividend'.

Shareholders are business stakeholders because they have a financial stake in a company. They expect a share of profits and, in the normal course of events, a rise in the value of the shares. They naturally hope that the company will make a big profit and be successful.

Companies hold shareholder meetings from time-to-time. Shareholders express their opinions in these meetings, sometimes strongly. These opinions reflect their interests as stakeholders. Shareholders often raise issues such as:

- the amount of profit made by the company
- the very high salaries in some cases paid to the directors of the company!
- the company's environmental policy

Companies also have to bear in mind the political views of their shareholders: there are sometimes shareholders' protests against the export of goods to countries where the workers are treated and paid badly.

Activity 4.3

Stakeholders
– shareholders

ASB's unhappy shareholders

The shareholders of ASB Holdings yesterday strongly criticised the company directors who were challenged by questions such as:

'How do you justify a 20% salary rise for yourselves when the dividend went down by over 5%?'

and

'How do you justify using hardwood timber imported from the rain forests of South America when you can use European timber? Do you realise the damage this is doing to the wildlife of the rainforests?'

The press report on the left tells the public what happened at a shareholder meeting of ASB, a UK furniture manufacturer.

1   Why should the shareholders object to the directors of ASB having large salary increases?

2   Why should the shareholders object to ASB importing hardwood timber from the South American rainforests?

the local community

The word 'community' can refer to the *local* community – your city area, town, village. It can also refer to the *national* community – the population of the UK (if you live in the UK).

The local community has an interest in business for a number of reasons:

- the local community needs full employment
- the local community looks to businesses to preserve and to clean up the environment
- businesses are an important source of support for events and charities
- businesses can have an influence on planning – deciding where to locate new factories or retail parks, for example

Businesses take account of these needs and pressures by offering employment. They also sponsor sporting and charitable events and help the environment by planting trees, recycling materials and cutting down on energy use.

Activity 4.4

Stakeholders
– the local community

Investigate local newspapers, local radio, TV and forms of advertising such as posters and leaflets for examples of the ways in which businesses are having an effect on the local community.

Write down examples you find of:

1   businesses providing new jobs

2   businesses helping to preserve the environment, eg by recycling materials, saving energy

3   businesses sponsoring events, eg sport and charities

Now write down reasons why you think these businesses can benefit from helping the local community in these ways.

the government

The government is also a stakeholder in business.

The government has an interest in and influence over business in a number of different ways . . .

businesses and the law

The government creates laws in Parliament. These affect the way that businesses operate.

Laws cover areas such as:

- planning permissions – where businesses can operate
- Health & Safety regulations – the way a business manages the safety of its premises and the health of its workforce
- employment law – the ways employees are treated – eg protection of the rights of part-timers, the prevention of racial and sexual discrimination

businesses and taxation

The government taxes businesses through the Inland Revenue, using the money raised to invest in areas such as transport and the Health Service.

Activity 4.5

Stakeholders

– the government

The newspaper headlines shown below are examples of ways in which the government influences businesses.

Write down how each of the headlines is likely to affect businesses.

Government increases level of minimum wage

Government reduces tax on diesel fuel

Government brings in new Health & Safety regulations

stakeholders and the size of the business

It is important to realise that the size of the business you are investigating will affect the number of stakeholders involved in that business. Generally speaking, the larger the business, the more stakeholders will have an interest in it.

A sole trader business, for example, will not have to worry about

- shareholders – there are none – the owner takes the profit
- employees – if it is a sole trader business there may be no employees
- the local community – the sole trader business is unlikely to make much impact here

The customer is the type of stakeholder the sole trader very much depends on. An upset customer is a customer lost!

If, on the other hand, the business is larger, a company like Tesco or BT for example, the whole range of stakeholders is likely to influence what the business does.

A larger business will be more in the public eye. If it upsets its customers or causes a major pollution scare, it becomes national news. Large companies often run a 'public relations' department which deals with the company's image in the eyes of the public.

Activity 4.6

Stakeholders

– how many stakeholders?

Ramjit Khan runs a taxi business with his brother Imran. They operate the business from home.

The Royal Bank of Scotland is a major UK bank. It is set up as a company and has branches throughout the UK.

1   Make a list of the stakeholders that are likely to have an interest in the Khan brothers' business.

2   Make a list of the stakeholders that are likely to have an interest in The Royal Bank of Scotland.

3   Write down why you think the two lists are different.

what have you learnt from this chapter?

● *Stakeholders are people who have an interest – a 'stake' – of some sort in a business.*

● *Customers are very important stakeholders, particularly when the business faces competition for its products. If the business keeps its customers happy it will retain those customers and stand a better chance of being successful.*

● *Employees and managers work inside the business and are also stakeholders. A well-run business will treat its employees well by providing good pay, training and job prospects. It will also provide rewards for successful managers.*

● *The shareholders of a company have a financial 'stake' in the business and will expect a share of the company's profits.*

● *The local community and environmental pressure groups have an interest in what businesses do to benefit the community. They also need to know that businesses are caring for the environment.*

● *The government has an interest as a stakeholder in businesses. It creates laws for the regulation of businesses and it collects taxes from businesses to pay for government spending.*

● *Different types of business have different types of stakeholder. It is usually true to say that the larger the business the greater the number of stakeholders.*

revision questions

1   List three types of stakeholder of a sole trader business.

2   List three types of stakeholder of a limited company business.

3   Fill in the spaces in the text using these words:

internal   external   shareholders   community

Customers are .... stakeholders and look for benefits like low prices. .... are .... stakeholders and look for the business to provide a return on their investment. The .... on the other hand expects a business to take care of the environment.

4   To which type of stakeholder is business profit most likely to be of the greatest interest? (Choose one answer from A,B,C & D).

A   a customer

B   a shareholder

C   the local community

D   the government

5   To which type of stakeholder is caring for the environment most likely to be of the greatest interest? (Choose one answer from A,B,C & D).

A   a customer

B   a shareholder

C   the local community

D   an employee

6   To which type of stakeholder is a cut in prices most likely to be of the greatest interest? (Choose one answer from A,B,C & D).

A   a customer

B   a shareholder

C   an employee

D   the government

How a business works

Unit 1: How a business works
What a business does; inside the business; functional areas

what this chapter is about

A business is set up to provide a product – it might be a manufactured product or it might be a service. A business needs to be organised into different areas of activity such as sales and finance so that it can provide this product. This chapter looks at how those different areas work together.

what you will learn from this chapter

- *All businesses have to organise themselves into different areas of activity – sales or finance, for example. These are known as functional areas – in other words areas in which different types of activity take place.*

- *The functions of a business include:*
  - *human resources – looking after the employees*
  - *finance – managing the money coming in and out*
  - *production – manufacturing a product or providing a service*
  - *marketing and sales – finding out what products the customers need and then selling the products to them*
  - *customer service – looking after the customers' needs (this is dealt with in Chapter 6, pages 87-90)*
  - *administration – providing all the backup needed (this is dealt with in Chapter 7, pages 103-106)*

- *Employees have different job titles, depending on what they do in the business.*

now read on . . .

functions in business

what does this mean?

A function in business is an area of activity in the business.

It does not matter if the business is a sole trader or a public limited company, the functions – areas of activity – remain the same, for example: buying and selling, dealing with customers, raising money, making sure there is soap in the cloakroom. Someone has got to do these tasks. It is up to the business to organise them in an efficient way.

different functional areas

You will see from the two Activities which follow that business activities can be classified in **functional areas**, even if the business is a sole trader who does everything himself or herself. The main functional areas are:

human resources	looking after the employees, for example keeping employee records, training and disciplining
finance	managing the money coming in and out, for example paying bills, paying wages, keeping the books
administration	providing all the backup needed – the day-to-day jobs that have to be done
production	manufacturing a product or providing a service
marketing and sales	finding out what products the customers need and selling those products to them
customer service	looking after the customers' needs, dealing with their complaints

Activity 5.1

Functional areas
Your school or college

Your own school or college is an organisation which in many ways is run along business lines. You are the customer and your education is the product.

Make a list of the functions which you can identify at work in your school or college.

Activity 5.2

Style on Top
A day in the life of Tina Solo

Tina Solo runs a busy town-centre hair salon 'Style on top' as a sole trader business. She employs four stylists and also works in the salon herself. She works a long day but the business is profitable and she enjoys it.

Tina's working day

08.00   Arrive at salon and open post.

08.15   Sketch out text for new advert to go in the local evening paper.

08.30   Talk to senior stylist Tracy about training of new assistant who started this week.

08.45   Try to pacify customer who rings up and wants an appointment that morning. They are fully booked until the afternoon. Customer not pleased. Manages to arrange a 15.00 appointment. The customer is happy in the end.

09.00   Salon opens. Talk to new assistant about her work and training.

09.30   Deal with bills – write out five cheques.

10.00   Work in salon, styling hair.

12.00   Have sandwiches and make telephone call to book advert in local paper.

12.15   Telephone accountant with a query about tax position of new employee. Is she to be put on an emergency code?

12.30   Have to have words with one stylist about the shoes she is wearing. They are not suitable for the job.

13.00   Back to work in salon, styling hair.

15.00   Have a ten minute chat with the new assistant during her coffee break – how is she getting on? Then back to work again in the salon.

17.00   Salon closing time. Door locked.

17.30   Salon alarm set. Go home.

19.00   Tina spends an hour at home writing up the cash book.

20.00   To the fitness centre for a workout. Suggest to a friend that she visits the salon for tinting.

activities

1   Draw up 6 columns on an A4 sheet of paper and head them up as follows:

human resources	finance	administration	production	marketing and sales	customer service
		08.00 Open post		08.15 Sketch out advert	

2   Go through the list of Tina's activities during the day and write each business activity in the appropriate column, together with the time it takes place. Two of the activities are already entered to give you a start.

3   Do all the business activities take place on the business premises? What does your answer tell you about the life of a sole trader?

departments in businesses

Tina in the last Activity was a sole trader who undertook most of the business functions herself. Many sole traders are able to cope with the workload of the back-up functions such as finance and human resources because the scale of their operations and the number of people they employ are limited.

If the workload gets too much it is always possible to pay someone else to do the specialised work. The sole trader could always employ a book-keeper to deal with the financial records or a bureau or an accountant to manage the payroll.

the need for departments

If the business is a large company with many employees, customers and suppliers, each business function is likely to be carried out by an individual department. There is no hard and fast rule about what the departments should be. It will all depend on the nature and size of the business. Set out on the next page is a diagram showing the departments which might be found in a manufacturing business.

departments in a manufacturing business

sales & marketing department

- market research - finding out customer needs
- promoting the product
- selling and distributing

customer services department

- providing information
- giving advice
- after-sales service
- dealing with complaints

human resources department

- recruiting staff
- training staff
- disciplining staff
- working conditions
- dealing with Health & Safety

finance department

- raising finance
- keeping accounts
- paying wages and salaries
- paying bills
- estimating future spending

administration department

- providing back-up services – filing, mailing, copying
- looking after the premises
- looking after equipment

production department

- organising the production line
- materials and equipment
- developing new products
- quality control

Activity 5.3

Which department?

Look at the departments shown in the diagram on the previous page and complete the sentences below with the name of the department you think fits the description. Copy out the headings and sentences for your portfolio, and head the sheet "Departments in a business."

1   .... Department

This department is concerned with the employees – it deals with training, recruitment, working conditions and disciplining staff.

2   .... Department

This department is mainly concerned with manufacturing products. Without this department no profit is likely to be made!

3   .... Department

This department must get the customers interested in purchasing the product – it must go and get the orders needed by the department in No 2 above.

4   .... Department

This department provides information and advice to customers; it deals with customer complaints and offers after-sales service.

5   .... Department

This department looks after the business premises and equipment; it provides back-up such as photocopying, filing and mailing.

6   .... Department

This department is concerned with keeping accounts, keeping an eye on the expenses incurred by the business, calculating wages, and paying bills.

the job ladder

When you investigate a business for your Assessment you will see that different jobs in departments have different pay, power and responsibility. The higher you progress in a business the more you are paid but the more responsibility you are given. Jobs in a company include:

- **director** – the person in overall charge of a department

- **manager** – the person who reports to the director and who is charge of the running and decision-making of the department; the manager will also be involved in planning

- **supervisor** – a person who reports to a manager and who oversees the day-to-day running of the department; the supervisor often works alongside the assistants

- **assistant** – a person who carries out the day-to-day activity of the business – working on a production line, selling a service, working a till – this is the starting point for most people getting a first job

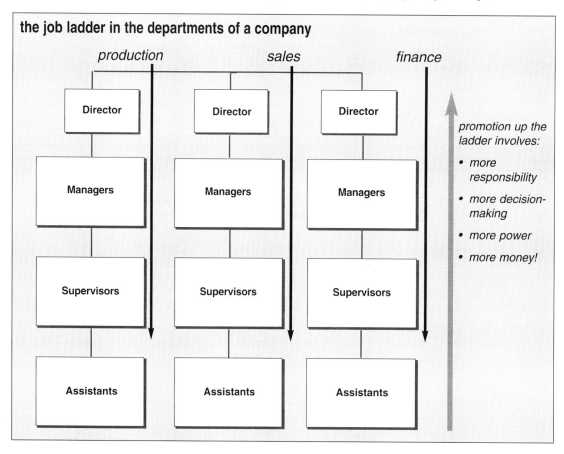

the job ladder in the departments of a company

production *sales* *finance*

| Director | Director | Director |

promotion up the ladder involves:

- *more responsibility*
- *more decision-making*
- *more power*
- *more money!*

| Managers | Managers | Managers |

| Supervisors | Supervisors | Supervisors |

| Assistants | Assistants | Assistants |

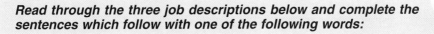

Activity 5.4

Types of job

Read through the three job descriptions below and complete the sentences which follow with one of the following words:

      assistant   *supervisor*   *manager*

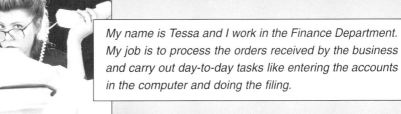

My name is Tessa and I work in the Finance Department. My job is to process the orders received by the business and carry out day-to-day tasks like entering the accounts in the computer and doing the filing.

My name is Bob. I have worked for the company for twenty five years. I am responsible for the running of the Production Department and report directly to the Production Director.

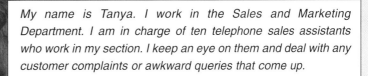

My name is Tanya. I work in the Sales and Marketing Department. I am in charge of ten telephone sales assistants who work in my section. I keep an eye on them and deal with any customer complaints or awkward queries that come up.

1   *Tessa is an* ....

2   *Bob is a* ....

3   *Tanya is a* ....

now read on to find out more about the work involved in different business functions . .

human resources department

jobs in 'human resources' and 'personnel'

Most organisations, apart from very small ones, have a Human Resources or 'Personnel' department or section. The role of the Human Resources function is to deal with employees. The term Human Resources is often shortened to 'HR'.

Human resources staff deal with a wide variety of tasks and have a number of areas of activity – all related to people. . .

recruitment

This involves:

- drawing up a 'job description' of the job that needs filling
- advertising the job
- holding interviews
- appointing the new employee and giving them a written contract or 'terms of employment'

keeping the employee – retention

Keeping the employee – 'retention' – is important for a business. This can be done by:

- paying good wages
- providing promotion prospects
- training and development
- providing pleasant working conditions
- varying the work

If an employee is not well treated, he or she will soon start looking for other employment.

discipline and dismissal

One of the less pleasant tasks of HR work is discipline and dismissal of employees. The important point for an employer to bear in mind when disciplining or dismissing an employee is to keep strictly to the procedures laid down by law.

If an employee fails to keep to these guidelines the disciplined or dismissed employee can use the help provided by employee organisations or Trade Unions to take the employer to an Employment Tribunal.

complying with employment law

The human resources function must make sure that the business complies with employment law, in particular

- not discriminating against employees because of their race

- not discriminating against employees because of their sex

The business must also comply with Health & Safety at Work regulations which set out rules for maintaining a safe and danger-free workplace.

how the human resources function is organised

Even in very small businesses any manager will include human resource management as one of his or her job roles. He or she will look after staff and deal with issues such as training and discipline.

In a large business the HR function will be carried out by a department which will have a wide variety of jobs, all carrying out different activities.

The diagram below shows a department that which is typical of a big company or local authority. In this case it belongs to Carcare Limited, a large company which makes car accessories and employs over 250 people.

How is the Human Resources department structured? Look at the chart below and then read the job roles for the names employees on the next few pages.

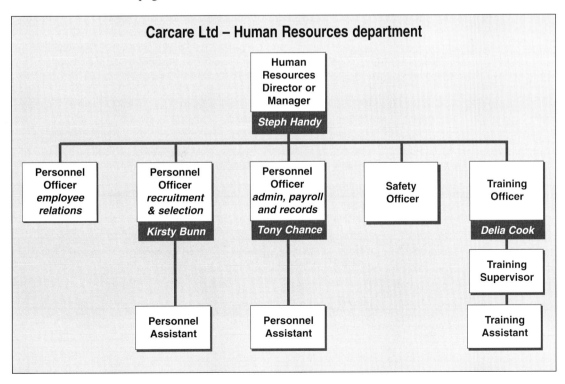

Jobs in the Human Resources Department of Carcare Limited

STEPH HANDY

HUMAN RESOURCES DIRECTOR

"I have worked for Carcare for 13 years, starting off as a personnel officer and then becoming personnel manager eight years ago. Three years later I was made a director of the company as well. My main roles include:

In the Human Resources department . . .

1   *Carrying out the instructions of the Managing Director.*

2   *Ensuring all my staff work effectively.*

3   *Ensuring my department reaches its targets. In this department last year our target was to reduce the level of sickness absence from 6.5 days lost per employee per year to 4 days. We actually got it down to 3.5!*

4   *Ensuring my staff are motivated so that they do their jobs properly and enjoy what they are doing.*

5   *Carrying out the administration of the department – this includes the supervision of my five section officers.*

Then for the company as a whole I have these jobs to do . . .

6   *Operating an effective communications system to ensure that all staff know what is going on .*

7   *Encouraging all our employees to say what they think and contribute ideas of their own (for example, when I was a personnel officer ten years ago I introduced a suggestion scheme which many of our employees have now used).*

8   *Ensuring that the company has a successful working relationship with all our employees."*

KIRSTY BUNN

PERSONNEL OFFICER - RECRUITMENT AND SELECTION

"My main job involves the recruitment and selection of the right quality and quantity of staff. Firstly I have to talk to departmental managers who want to replace staff or recruit extra staff. They have to tell me exactly what they are looking for. I have to write out the job adverts and place them in the newspapers and at the job centres. Then I have to choose candidates to interview, often from hundreds of applications, and then invite them over for a "selection day". Steph (my manager) believes that it is too unreliable just to rely on a job interview so she expects all candidates invited in to do a series of job-related tests. Luckily, my personnel assistant, Sarah, sorts all that out."

TONY CHANCE

PERSONNEL OFFICER - ADMINISTRATION, PAYROLL AND RECORDS

"I used to be a factory assembly worker but had to give that up fifteen years ago after a factory accident that permanently damaged my left arm. My job includes putting all newcomers onto the computerised payroll system and sorting out the pay arrangements for leavers. I handle all queries and complaints from staff about pay and I deal with the appropriate person in the company accounts department. I look after all the personnel records, including holidays and sickness."

DELIA COOK

TRAINING OFFICER

"To carry out my role I have a Training Supervisor and Training Assistant to help me. My main role is the development and training of staff. My main concern is employee development. This means making sure that:

1   Staff are motivated to perform as well as they possibly can.

2   The organisation makes the best use of everyone's skills and abilities.

the finance department

finance and other function areas

The finance function in a business is closely involved with the production of goods and services and so links up with other function areas in the business. Just as human resources is concerned with people, finance is concerned with money. Money is the oil that keeps the wheels of the business turning; without it the business seizes up.

Finance is principally concerned with:

*   the keeping of accounts
*   raising money for the business
*   paying wages and salaries

keeping accounts

Later in this book (Chapter 10) we will be looking in detail at the financial documents involved in buying and selling. These documents form the first part of a process which ends up with the production of financial reports such as profit statements.

Financial transactions of all types are recorded in accounts. In most accounting systems there will be separate accounts for:

*   sales and purchases
*   each type of expense
*   debtors (people who owe the business money)
*   creditors (people to whom the business owes money)

These accounts are recorded in books known as ledgers. The ledgers can be written in by hand, or they can be computerised. If you use a computer accounting program, you input the transactions into the computer where they are stored on disk. The screen below shows a payment for some stationery bought by the business.

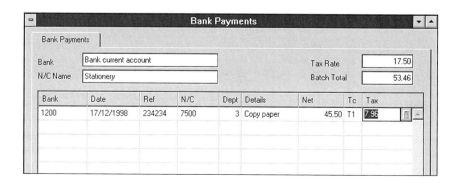

payroll

Payroll is the function in the business which works out the wages and salaries and deductions (income tax and National Insurance) of its employees. Payroll can either be done by hand using the forms and instructions provided by the Inland Revenue, or it can be done by computer.

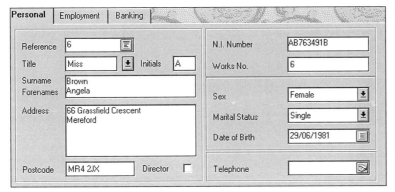

More and more businesses are now using computer payroll programs as they are faster and very accurate.

The screen on the left shows an employee record on a computer payroll program.

obtaining capital and resources

Money is the lifeblood of any business. Money is required by a business for:

- *long-term needs* such as investing in premises, machinery, computers
- *short-term needs* such as buying stock and raw materials, paying bills, paying wages

It is the job of the Finance Department to organise the raising of money for the different function areas of the business.

Money can be provided by the owner of the business – this is known as 'capital'. It can also be borrowed from the bank.

The finance raised is normally either short-term or long-term. Look at the diagram below.

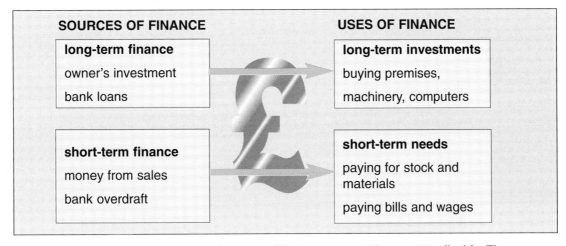

SOURCES OF FINANCE	USES OF FINANCE
long-term finance owner's investment bank loans	**long-term investments** buying premises, machinery, computers
short-term finance money from sales bank overdraft	**short-term needs** paying for stock and materials paying bills and wages

now read about the sort of jobs you would expect to find in Finance . . .

Jobs in the Finance Department of Carcare Limited, manufacturer of car accessories

KERRY SMITH

PAYROLL ASSISTANT

"I work as a wages clerk in the finance office. There are ten clerks altogether, and our supervisor.

Although we occasionally have to work out wages manually, most jobs are computerised now – all we have to do is to enter the hours worked by each employee on the computer, and it automatically works out the pay and prints out a payslip. I find the work interesting because I like working with figures."

NIGEL BURTON

CREDIT CONTROLLER

"I work at a supervisory level. My job in basic terms is to make sure that customers we sell to on credit will pay up. These customers are mostly shops and garages. The big shops are normally no trouble, but the smaller businesses often get into difficulties and the first we know about it is that they don't pay their bills. I have five assistants working under me. The job is an important one because if our customers don't pay up they become bad debts and the business loses money as a result. Our computer system printouts an 'aged debtor' report each week – this shows up any overdue accounts. We soon get onto them I can tell you."

JOHN CARDWELL

SALES LEDGER CLERK

"My main job is issuing invoices to customers who order goods from us. I have to check their purchase order forms carefully and also make sure they are good accounts and not bad payers. We used to type out the invoices ourselves but we now have a computer system which prints them out in batches. The computer does all the calculations, which is great, but we still have to check our work carefully."

the production department

what is production?

'Production' is the process which turns resources into a product – a manufactured item or a service – which can be sold by the business.

Look at the resources needed by a manufacturer . . .

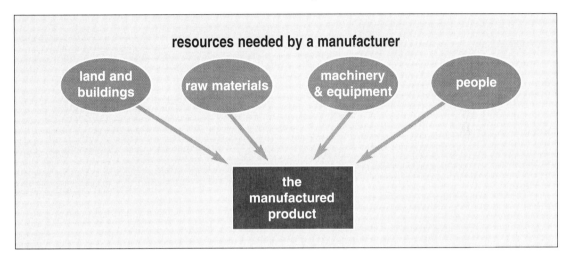

Now look at the resources needed by a food supermarket. . . the product here is the goods sold to the public . . .

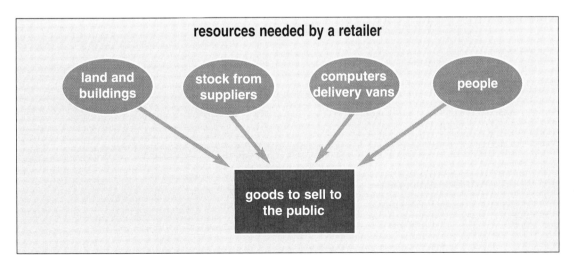

The Case Study on the next page shows the stages in the production of Cadburys milk chocolate.

Case Study

Production of **Cadbury's** Dairy Milk chocolate bars

computer control of the production line

chocolate being mixed

formed into slabs – on the production line

. . . being wrapped

---

points for class discussion

What part does machinery play in the production of chocolate?

What other products would be suited to this method of production?

jobs in production

Production covers a wide range of jobs. Remember too that production does not just mean manufacture – production is the process of producing any product, including a service. The department in a service business which organises the resources needed is often known as the 'operations department'. People working in production therefore include:

- production line operators
- production supervisors and managers
- support staff
- specialist staff – for example people researching in to new products

Two jobs are described below . . .

Jobs in the Production Department of Carcare Limited, manufacturer of car accessories

SEAN O'CASEY

PRODUCTION MANAGER

"I am in charge of the production lines of the business. I report directly to the production director. I also work with Rick Brunson, the sales manager, who lets me know about any problems. I also talk regularly with other departmental managers – particularly the purchasing manager who buys in all my raw materials and components. I also deal with the Finance Manager who keeps an eye on cost levels and discusses production budgets with me on a regular basis.

I am in charge of 150 production line workers. We are a fairly happy bunch – we rarely have any disputes. Carcare is a good employer and looks after its workforce."

JANINE LEGRAS

PRODUCTION LINE EMPLOYEE

"I have worked on the production lines here at Carcare for two years now. At the moment I make the covers for car seats. They like women on this job because you have to be nimble-fingered. There are twenty of us on this line, and a supervisor who keeps her eye on us and the work we do."

the sales and marketing function

The marketing of a product follows a number of stages. These apply equally if the product is a manufactured item like a car or a service like a holiday. Study these stages in the diagram below. The most important stages are:

- **market research** – finding out what the customer needs
- **promotion** – making sure the customer knows about the product
- **selling** – getting the customer to buy the product

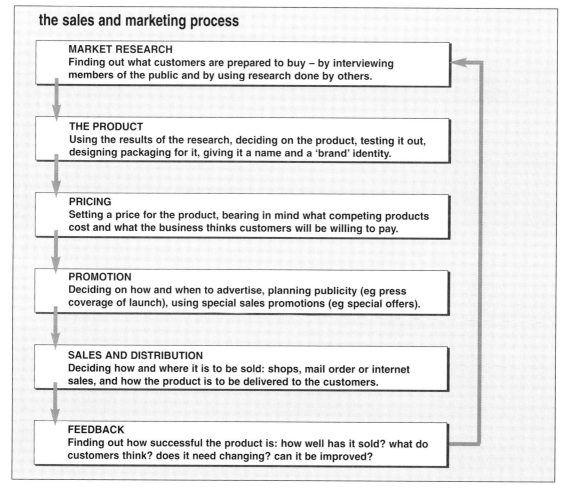

the sales and marketing process

MARKET RESEARCH
Finding out what customers are prepared to buy – by interviewing members of the public and by using research done by others.

THE PRODUCT
Using the results of the research, deciding on the product, testing it out, designing packaging for it, giving it a name and a 'brand' identity.

PRICING
Setting a price for the product, bearing in mind what competing products cost and what the business thinks customers will be willing to pay.

PROMOTION
Deciding on how and when to advertise, planning publicity (eg press coverage of launch), using special sales promotions (eg special offers).

SALES AND DISTRIBUTION
Deciding how and where it is to be sold: shops, mail order or internet sales, and how the product is to be delivered to the customers.

FEEDBACK
Finding out how successful the product is: how well has it sold? what do customers think? does it need changing? can it be improved?

market research

Market research means finding out:

- what types of customer are in the market place
- what products those customers want

Businesses can carry out research in two main ways:

- they can look at research work done already
- they can go out and find out for themselves by asking customers questions in surveys – in the street or over the telephone

Customers are often divided up into 'types' by age, by sex and by the amount of money they have. You will be able to think of products which appeal to

- men – cars
- women – cosmetics
- young people – fashion clothes
- older people – cruise holidays
- very well-off people – expensive watches

promotion

When a business has decided what product to produce, it needs to *promote* it to its customers. This can involve advertising, sponsorship, and getting the product on the news.

selling

Direct sales are made when the provider of the product sells direct to the consumer without any middle person such as an agent or wholesaler being involved. Remember that a product can be a manufactured item or a service.

Indirect sales are made when the provider of the product sells to the consumer through a middle person.

Look at the diagrams and the examples :

direct selling

Examples:

- a taxi takes you to the station
- you buy a book direct from our website www.osbornebooks.co.uk

indirect selling

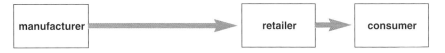

Example: you buy a box of Kelloggs Cornflakes from Asda.

There are also other sales methods you will come across . . .

direct mail

Businesses obtain databases of names and addresses and send catalogues to selected types of customers so that they can buy direct by mail order. This method is used both for selling to the public and to other businesses. Much of this sort of sales material can end up in the bin!

telesales

Selling by telephoning the customer direct – telesales – has become very common, both when selling to the public and to other businesses. It is used extensively by organisations like double-glazing firms.

e-commerce

Selling through websites is now the fastest growing sales method worldwide. Manufacturers and mail order companies are easily accessed on-line and through net 'searches'. Popular products sold using this method include books, CDs, cars and holidays. If you have access to the internet try the on-line bookstore www. amazon.co.uk or shopping sites available through the web search engines such as www. yahoo.co.uk

job roles in marketing and sales

The job descriptions below and on the next page show the types of marketing and sales jobs available in Carcare Limited.

Jobs in the Sales & Marketing Department of Carcare Limited, manufacturer of car accessories

FRANK HANCOCK, SALES AND MARKETING DIRECTOR

"I am in charge of all of the marketing sections, such as marketing research, promotion, sales and the distribution of goods. All of the managers of these sections meet with me regularly. All in all there are about thirty people working for me.

Once a month I discuss company policy at a board meeting with the managing director, (my boss), and the directors of production, human resources and finance so that we can plan ahead and decide where the whole company is going."

JANE SEYMOUR,

MARKETING RESEARCH MANAGER

"I am responsible for finding out what the public thinks about our products, and what they want in the future. My staff do this by looking at the way our products and those of our competitors have sold in the past, and asking questions about consumer opinions, usually using questionnaires. All this information is collected and analysed so that I can make recommendations to the Sales and Marketing Director about the future. We call this forecasting.

Sometimes we do industrial research into what the 'trade' thinks. This means asking the retailers we sell to for their opinions, about our products, our advertising, and our delivery service. You see, marketing research looks at everything we do. This gives my job great variety, and my staff are not doing the same things every day. I have six people working for me directly, although if we have a big job to do I might go to an outside research agency for help."

JANE PENTRY, SALES ASSISTANT

"I work in Sales Department. I need to know all about the products so that I can explain things to the customers. I have had sales training with the company and I now understand the importance of listening to the customer rather than just talking at him or her. I get a real buzz from gaining a sale.

Next month I will move to another department for more experience. This is hard work but I need to widen my experience if I want to gain promotion to being a supervisor."

what have you learnt from this chapter?

- All businesses involve different areas of activity which are known as functional areas – these are parts of the business in which different types of activity such as sales or finance take place.

- A functional area can be just one job or it can be a whole department – it all depends on this size of the business.

- Larger businesses, such as the ones you are investigating, are likely to have departments for

  human resources – recruiting and looking after the employees and disciplining them or even dismissing them

  finance – managing the money coming in and out – keeping accounts, paying the wages and raising money for the business

  production – managing the resources for manufacturing a product or providing a service

  marketing and sales – finding out what products the customers need, promoting them and then selling the products to them

  customer service – looking after the customers' needs (this is dealt with in the next chapter)

  administration – providing all the backup needed (this is dealt with in Chapter 7)

- Employees have different job titles, depending on what they do in the business. The most common types are:

  manager – a person who is responsible for and is in charge of a department – he or she plans and makes major decisions

  supervisor – a person who reports to the manager and is in charge of the day-to-day running of a department and oversees the assistants

  assistant – a person who carries out the day-to-day work of the business and is looked after by a supervisor

revision questions

Fill in the spaces in the numbered sentences below using these words:

human resources   **sales and marketing**

finance   **production**

administration   **customer service**

1 Recruitment of employees is carried out by ....
.... department.

2 Maintenance of the production line is carried out by
.... department.

3 Maintenance of the premises is carried out by ....
department.

4 Advertising of the products of the business is carried out by
.... department.

5 Dealing with customer complaints is carried out by
.... department.

6 Paying the wages is carried out by ....
department.

7 Dismissal of staff is carried out by ....
....department.

8 Account books are kept by .... department.

9 Asking the public for new products that they need is carried out by
.... department.

10 The design and development of new products is carried out by
.... department.

6 Looking after customers

what this chapter is about

Customers are important to businesses and so businesses need to look after their customers. This involves what is known as 'customer care' and 'customer service'. This is another of the functional areas of a business. This chapter looks at the activities involved in 'customer care' and 'customer service'.

what you will learn from this chapter

- *Businesses need to keep their customers happy by providing a range of services for them:*
  - *providing information – knowing the products*
  - *giving advice – undertstanding the customer and selling the 'right' product*
  - *providing a high level of 'customer care' – looking after the customer and providing what the customer expects*
  - *proving after-sales service*

- *There are many different types of customer – individuals and other businesses, for example*

- *Employees involved in sales need to know how 'to sell' the product and how the 'clinch' the sale. This process involves finding out what the customer needs and then providing the customer with information about the product, ways to pay, and the guarantee that covers the product.*

- *Employees involved in selling need to know about the various consumer laws which cover selling goods and services.*

now read on . . .

customer service

what you need to study in this chapter

This chapter is mainly written to cover the topic of customer service needed for your Assessment for Unit 1 'How a business works'. It also provides the material you need for Option Unit 5 'Looking after customers'.

what is customer service?

Businesses need their customers to buy their products or to use their services in order to survive and make a profit. The way that they treat their customers is therefore very important. Many businesses have a policy of 'customer service' which involves putting the customer first in all situations. Customer service involves:

- making sure the product range is available to the customer
- making sure the product range can be delivered if necessary
- making sure the product is safe and reliable
- providing information about products and being able to give advice
- providing credit facilities where appropriate (allowing the customer to pay over a period of time)
- providing after-sales service – guarantees, spare parts, help-lines

It should be the aim of every business to provide the highest level of customer service.

There are laws which provide protection to consumers buying products. Businesses should know what customers' rights are under these laws; it will help them maintain customer service.

why is customer service so important?

The first impression of a customer dealing with an organisation – whether as a shopper, a visitor or when speaking over the telephone – is based on the level of customer service he or she receives. Is the person who deals with the customer polite and helpful, or is the person unhelpful and not interested in the customer's request? The result will be a good impression – or a bad impression – of the whole organisation. If the impression is good, the person will want to do business again; if the impression is bad, the organisation will probably have lost a customer for good. Many organisations have a customer service department, and shops often have a customer services desk, as shown in the picture on the next page.

a customer services desk

customer care

Customer care puts customer service into operation. If you get a part-time job in an organisation or a work placement, you may have to deal with customers, over a counter, at a reception desk, over the telephone, or elsewhere on the premises. Many business organisations run special customer care training programmes, spending much time and money ensuring that their employees provide a high level of customer service.

What is a customer care scheme? It concentrates the whole business on the needs of the customer rather than the needs of the business or the employee. It is an attitude which should run through the whole organisation from the managing director to the most junior sales assistant.

customer service at work

Customer service should be provided wherever the customer meets the business organisation: over the counter, or on the telephone. There are many examples of job roles involving customer service:

- shop assistants

- doctors' receptionists

- bank assistants

- bus drivers

- swimming pool attendants

- telephone sales staff (mail order firms)

Activity 6.1

Customer service at work how successful is it?

Over a period of two or three days (a weekend for example) carry out a survey of the situations where you were a customer of a business organisation (eg a taking a taxi ride, going to a cinema, buying a drink).

Choose two of the situations. One should be the <u>best</u> example of customer care and the other the <u>worst</u> example.

1   Write notes on the two situations, explaining:

– what was good about the best example of customer care

– what was bad about the worst example of customer care

2   Write a list of five 'hints' on good customer care to give to a person (like a sales assistant) who deals with the public.

the need for information and advice

Many customers need information and advice. They may be about to make a purchase, or they may just be 'shopping around' for a product and looking for the best price or after-sales service. Whatever the situation the sales assistant must:

know the product range

Know the price, product description, availability, and details of after-sales service (guarantees and policy on 'money back'). Knowing the product ideally also means knowing the competitor's product: 'Oh yes, I know they are cheaper at Underwoods, but look at the quality we have here – this will last a long time.' The assistant must, however, beware of making false or over-ambitious claims: the customer will soon see through them.

know other sources of information

If the assistant is unable to provide all the information required, someone else in (or outside) the organisation may be able to help the customer. For example the question may be very technical: 'Will this hair dryer work off the mains electricity supply in Kuwait?' The question may have to be referred to the technical department of the manufacturer. The customer will not necessarily expect the shop assistant to know the answer, but may be very unhappy if the assistant does not know how to find out.

Some customers do not just need information, they need very specific assistance. The shop assistant in a department store, for example, should be prepared to point out where the toilets are, where the coffee shop is, or where the childrens' play area is located. They should also have the skills necessary for the area in which they work, eg measuring feet for shoes.

the need for care

Apart from the obvious use of customer care skills, employees should be able to 'care' for customers when they get into trouble. 'Care' is more than 'help'; it means thinking in advance about a customer's needs. Consider the following examples:

- a sales assistant sees that a pregnant woman is exhausted with tramping around the shops and provides her with a chair to sit down on

- a sales assistant sees that an elderly lady is confused and tired, and spends more time serving the lady and helping her to make simple decisions

In all these cases, the employee goes out of his or her way to provide care for the shopper, who will then think of the organisation in a good light.

customer care for business customers

So far in this chapter we have looked at individual customers – people out shopping, for example. It is important to realise that many businesses also sell to businesses. Examples include office stationery firms and businesses that make packaging. Customer care for businesses involves some additional factors . . .

price and discounts

Businesses who buy regularly or in bulk from their suppliers will expect special terms in return for their loyalty as customers. This normally involves what is known as 'trade discount' – a percentage reduction in price. See page 165 to see how this affects the financial documents which cover the sale.

delivery

Businesses will normally expect free delivery of the goods that they order. They also expect delivery on schedule. Suppliers that supply late or who send incorrect goods are suppliers that get dropped!

payment period

Businesses normally pay for supplies well after delivery – sometimes up to 90 days later. Suppliers that allow payment this late prove very popular.

customer types – individuals

We have already seen how different customers have different needs. Every employee providing customer service should be able to think carefully about these needs. There are many different types of customer, for example:

- the customer who needs information and advice
- the child
- 'special needs' customers, eg people in wheelchairs, blind customers

We have dealt with the person who needs information and advice (see page 89). We will now look at the child and the special needs customer.

the child

Ask any parent, nanny or child-minder and you will find that taking children shopping, or placing them in any situation which involves waiting, can be a considerable problem! Of course, some children are not a problem, and a smiling face normally means that everyone can relax.

If you are working in a business and are dealing with the public, you may encounter the following problems with children:

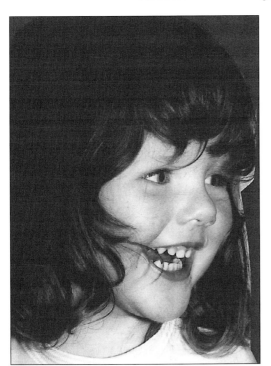

- children disrupting the course of business – creating a disturbance, destroying displays of goods
- children helping themselves to goods, tampering with telephone equipment
- lost children
- children trying to pay for goods

Whatever the situation, remember that it is the person in charge of the child who is responsible and who will have to be approached in the first instance if there is a problem. Only if there is a threat to safety – eg a lost child or a collapsing display – should you take direct action.

You should be sympathetic in situations where 'care' is needed – eg a distressed or bored child – you may be able to help the parent in a difficult situation. Through this you should get a satisfied customer.

special needs customers

Customers with special needs include:

the physically handicapped and disabled

People in wheelchairs and with walking frames will need special treatment and patience; the organisation should be equipped with suitable lifts and ramps.

the mentally handicapped

People who are slower than normal in carrying out the simplest transaction will need a high degree of care and understanding. Do not treat them disrespectfully.

the deaf ('hearing-impaired')

Some customers may be completely or partially deaf and will be skilled in lip reading and may be equipped with hearing aids. Do not shout at them.

the blind ('visually-impaired')

Blind people will be used to getting about in public, so ask them if they need help. Talk to them. There is nothing more frightening than being grabbed unexpectedly by a complete stranger, however well-meaning that person may be.

Activity 6.2

Customer service
dealing with the customers

You work as a shop assistant in a large store. How would you deal with the following customers?

1   *You suspect a three year-old child of taking and slipping a Mars bar into her mother's shopping bag.*

2   *A blind person approaches you and asks for a Robbie Williams CD. The home entertainment department is on the next floor.*

3   *You are covering for a colleague at lunch and are serving in a department which you do not know very well. A customer asks you a technical question about a product and you do not know the answer.*

4   *A man drops a bag and smashes a bottle of drink. It leaks out all over the floor which has a smooth tiled surface.*

5   *A man comes in singing. From his breath you realise that he has been drinking heavily.*

providing credit

A customer who is given *credit* is a customer who is supplied with an item or a service and is then allowed to pay at a later date. This is common practice in business-to-business dealings. When a business sells to the public – eg a shop selling a product to a customer – it normally expects immediate payment, unless a credit card (or shop card) is used.

credit cards and shop cards

A credit card is a plastic card which allows you to buy goods and services and pay for them later when you get your statement from the credit card company. If you do not settle up the full amount of the statement by a given date you will be charged interest on the amount you still owe. Interest is an extra amount which is charged when you borrow money.

The credit card can either be a general credit card, eg Visa or Mastercard, which can be used anywhere, or you can apply for a shop credit card which can only be used at that particular shop. A shop card may give you extra benefits such as discount on what you buy and previews of their Sales.

The card shown on the left is a Visa card issued by Barclays Bank. It can be used in most outlets worldwide.

Activity 6.3

Customer service
the benefits of credit

*Investigate **one** type of general credit card (eg a Visa card or a Mastercard) and **one** type of shop credit card. Collect leaflets about the cards if you can.*

1   *List <u>two</u> main benefits of the general credit card.*

2   *List <u>two</u> main benefits of the shop card.*

3   *Write down the reason why you think shops try to get customers to apply for a shop card.*

making the sale

selling methods

If you mention 'selling' to someone, they will probably think of number of different ways of selling:

- a sales assistant selling goods in a shop
- a door-to-door sales rep calling at your house
- telephone sales – someone selling double-glazing, for example

These all involve a person trying to convince you that you will be better off with their product.

Most people working in sales will have training in how to 'clinch' a sale. People selling over the telephone often have a script they have to work to.

selling in stages

Selling involves a number of different stages, all of which are designed to get the customer to buy the product.

Study the diagram below and read the case study which follows.

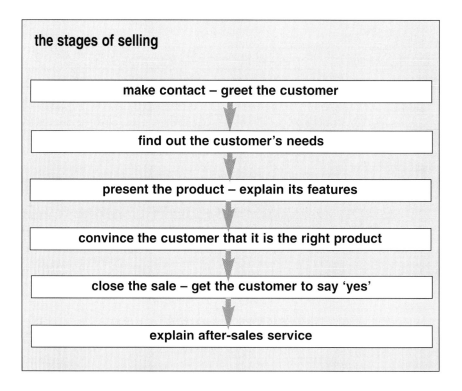

the stages of selling

make contact – greet the customer

find out the customer's needs

present the product – explain its features

convince the customer that it is the right product

close the sale – get the customer to say 'yes'

explain after-sales service

Case Study

Selling the mobile phone

> **situation**
>
> Sam works in Televox, a store which sells a wide range of mobile phone equipment.
>
> Tom comes to the counter and starts looking at the phones on display.
>
> How should Sam deal with the situation?
>
> What stages will he have to take Tom through to get his sale?

stage 1

make contact with the customer

Sam the salesman will make contact with Tom by greeting him politely: Sam has been on a sales training course at Televox which taught him the type of greeting to use.

"Good morning, Sir. How can I help you?"

stage 2

find out the customer's needs

Sam will need to find out what the customer is looking for:

"Is there any particular product you are interested in?"

"Yes, I would like to find out about mobile phones."

stage 3

present the product and explain its features

Sam the salesman will show Tom a number of models and must communicate to him a number of features:

- **the purpose and features** of each phone – what they will actually do and how they work

- **the price** of each phone

- **the unique selling point** (USP) of each phone – the feature which no other product possesses – the feature which makes it a 'must' and a product the customer has to buy

The conversation may well include the phrases quoted below. In each case note how Sam stresses the benefits to the customer.

the purpose of the product

"The phone will enable you to keep in touch with your friends and colleagues."

"It will enable you to access the internet anywhere and at any time."

explaining features

"This model has games as well as so will keep you entertained."

"This model has longer battery life than most other phones and so will not let you down."

the mention of price

"This phone has many features and is very good value at £69.95."

"We have a special offer on this one – it is reduced from £79.95 to £59.95 for this month only."

the unique selling point (USP)

"The Sportvox model is the only one on the market which is totally weatherproof and shockproof."

stage 4

answer questions and overcome doubts

Sam will answer Tom's questions, either while he is explaining the features, or after he has presented all the facts. This is an excellent opportunity for finding out exactly what the customer's needs are. Often a customer will have doubts about a product, or even objections. The successful salesperson will turn these to advantage and persuade the customer to make a purchase by explaining all the benefits of the product. The customer's questions may well cover the following areas:

- *how can I pay?*

- *after-sales service – can I get a refund if I am not happy with the product?*

- *what guarantee is there if the product goes wrong?*

- *is the product safe?*

Now read the following conversation, and see how the salesman turns questions into opportunities for stressing benefits and satisfying customer needs.

customer	"How can I pay for the phone? I am rather short of cash at the moment. I doubt if I can afford it."
salesman	"No problem. As long as you are over 18, we can offer you finance which allows you to make payment by easy repayments over up to three years."
customer	"That sounds a good idea. Another question I have is this: what is your after-sales service? What happens if there is anything wrong with the phone? Will you replace it? Will it have to go in for repair?"
salesman	"You won't have to worry about that. We offer a replacement or 'money back if not satisfied' service."
customer	"What about a guarantee then? These things often go wrong after a year or so."
salesman	"In return for a small payment we offer a three year extended guarantee which covers defects in the equipment – all labour and spare parts will be paid for if it goes wrong."
customer	"How do I know the phone is safe to use?"
salesman	"All products sold here comply with British Standards safety regulations."
customer	"Tell me about the Sportvox model again."

Sam (the salesman) can now assess whether Tom (the customer) is ready to make a decision to buy – he is ready to 'close the sale'.

stage 5

is the customer ready to make a decision?

The salesman can often tell from the customer's face whether he or she is keen to buy the product, or whether he or she just wants to beat a retreat out of the shop!

If the facial expressions are not so clear, certain phrases indicate that the customer is ready to say 'yes' to the product:

"That sounds a good idea."

"Tell me about the Sportvox model again."

stage 6

close the sale

The time has come for the salesman to clinch the deal. He can sense that the customer wants to make a 'yes' decision, or is on the verge of that decision.

The salesman will make comments which assume that the customer has made a 'yes' decision. The customer will then probably have no alternative but to buy! The salesman will say, for example:

"So the Sportvox is the model you would like. Do you need a carrying case?"

"Are you paying cash, or would you like to take our low-cost finance?"

"Would you like to see details of our extended guarantee scheme?"

The sale is then made.

customer rights and consumer law

One important job carried out by customer services staff is dealing with complaints. It is important that the staff know about the rights of customers when they buy goods or services. Sales staff will not be required to have a detailed knowledge of the law – they will need to know how to answer customers' questions and avoid saying the wrong thing! What are the main laws?

Trade Descriptions Act

The Trade Descriptions Act makes it a criminal offence:

- to make false statements about goods offered for sale
- to make misleading statements about services

Examples of offences include:

- stating that a car for sale has clocked up 15,000 miles, when in fact the figure is 35,000 miles
- making a misleading statement about a service, eg 'our dry cleaning is guaranteed to remove every stain' when it does not, or 'our apartments are within easy reach of the sea' when they are fifteen miles away

Sale of Goods Act

This Act states that you are entitled to expect any goods that you buy from a shop to be:

of 'satisfactory quality'
This means they must meet the standard that a 'reasonable' person would expect given the description and the price

'fit for the purpose'
The goods must do what they are supposed to do, or what the shop claims they can do: an umbrella should keep the rain out, a watch should keep accurate time.

'as described'
The goods must be what they are claimed to be: a 'leather coat' must be made of leather, a 'stereo TV' must provide stereo sound.

If any of these three above conditions is not met, the consumer is entitled to a full or a part refund, depending on how soon the fault appears, how serious it is and how quickly the matter is taken up.

For further information about consumer rights, log onto www.oft.gov.uk

food safety, weights and measures

Businesses that sell food are bound by **The Food Safety Act** which aims to make sure that food and drink is safe when it is bought. These regulations affect the ingredients of the food and the way in which it is prepared or cooked. They also prohibit any additives which are 'injurious to health'.

Businesses that sell products by measure – whether it be drinks at a bar or maggots in a fishing shop – are ruled by the **Weights and Measures Act**. Any business that gives 'short' measure is committing a criminal offence and can be prosecuted.

Activity 6.4

Customer service
legal protection for customers

Describe how the law protects a customer in each of the following situations. Include the name of the law in your explanations.

1   *A customer buys an umbrella which leaks in the rain.*

2   *An antique shop labels a chrome-plated tray as a 'silver' tray.*

3   *A food processing plant uses a preservative which has been banned.*

4   *A 250ml pot of cream from a dairy is found to contain only 230ml of cream.*

what have you learnt from this chapter?

● *Customers are important to businesses because businesses rely on them for sales and profit.*

● *Customer service means the idea of looking after customers and putting the customer first.*

● *Customer care is a scheme run by a business which concentrates the whole business on the needs of the customer.*

● *Customer service means:*
  - *providing information – knowing the products that you sell*
  - *giving advice – undertstanding the customer and selling the 'right' product*
  - *providing a high level of 'customer care' – looking after the customer and providing what the customer expects*
  - *proving after-sales service*

● *Business customers need customer service as much as individual customers do. Their needs are:*
  - *good prices and generous discounts*
  - *reliable and fast delivery*
  - *being able to pay a long time after the goods have been delivered*

● *Individual customers include not only ordinary purchasers but also customers with special needs and requirements, for example children and disabled customers.*

● *Part of customer service is the giving of credit, normally through credit cards. A credit card enables a customer to buy goods and services and to pay for them at a later date.*

● *Employees involved in sales need to know how 'to sell' the product and how the 'close' the sale. The stages of this process include finding out what the customer needs and, providing the customer with information about the product and then persuading them to buy.*

● *Employees involved in customer services need to know about the various consumer laws which cover selling goods and services.*

revision questions

Fill in the spaces in the text below below using these words:

> **providing information**   **after-sales**
>
> **giving advice**   **first**
>
> **credit card**   **closing**
>
> **needs**   **law**
>
> **stages**

The most important idea of customer service is putting the customer ....

Customer care involves the business ....

and .... to the customer; so

it is important that a sales assistant knows the features of the products well.

Sometimes a customer with special .... will need to be dealt

with. This situation will require special care and attention.

Selling is a skill and involves a number of .... which , if

successful, lead up to the sales assistant .... the sale.

Some customers will not be able to pay for goods or services straightaway. If

this is a problem, they can always use a ....

Another aspect of customer service is providing guarantees. This is part of

... service.

Of course, some customers will always complain. In many cases they are

protected by consumer ....

7

Administration and communication

Unit 1: How a business works – administration; working together – business communications

what this chapter is about

Businesses need two basic support systems which will enable them to operate smoothly and efficiently – good administration and good communication. Administration means making sure that the right resources are in the right place at the right time. Communication means making sure that the right information gets to the right place at the right time.

what you will learn from this chapter

● *Administration is a functional area which provides such back-up as:*

* *dealing with the post and e-mail*
* *keeping the records of the business up-to-date*
* *dealing with enquiries*
* *setting up meetings*
* *looking after the premises – eg cleaning and security*

● *There are a number of ways business employees can communicate with other employees and also with people outside the business:*

* *by word of mouth – by telephone, in meetings, in interviews*
* *in writing – memos, letters, messages, adverts, notices*
* *using information technology, for example e-mail (inside and outside the business), fax*

● *Efficient communication is important when dealing with people outside the business, eg customers, suppliers and the public.*

now read on . . .

administration – organising the work flow

all in a day's work

Whatever the size of a business, it is likely to have to deal with incoming, outgoing and internal communications. A sole trader is likely at times to have to work hard to manage to keep up with all that is going on. A larger business (such as the one you will be studying for your assessment) will need to be organised to deal with the flow of communications and also to provide all the back-up needed for the different business functions.

incoming

Information and messages – enquiries, orders, complaints – will come into the business by post, by fax, by phone and internet. Callers with appointments will arrive, callers without appointments will arrive.

outgoing

The business will also need to generate messages and information for external use – letters, quotes, catalogues, adverts, telesales – using a wide range of communication methods. It will also need to deliver its product – which may be an item or a service.

internal

The different functions within the business (eg sales, finance, production) need to communicate with each other in the day-to-day running of the organisation. The methods used can include paper documents, telephone, fax, intranet (internal e-mail) and meetings.

what is administration?

Clearly many of the activities listed above will be organised within the departments concerned and will be overseen by supervisors and managed by managers. For example a sales department will process orders received and the finance department is likely to process the payroll.

But there will be activities which do not *have* to be done within a specific department. These include:

- distributing the post when it arrives
- collecting and stamping the post going out at the end of the day
- operating the telephone switchboard
- dealing with callers to the premises
- photocopying and design and production of forms
- filing and database maintenance
- making sure the premises are clean and secure
- maintaining equipment such as computers

These activities are best described as 'back-up', and this is what we mean by 'administration' – making sure that the right resources are in the right place at the right time.

Activity 7.1

Administration
at your school or college

Find out what department or section is responsible for the following activities in your school or college.

1   dealing with the post – incoming and outgoing

2   processing all the photocopying and teaching aids needed by teachers

3   dealing with visitors during the day

4   operating the telephone switchboard

5   cleaning the premises

6   making sure all the computers are working correctly

how to organise the administration function

There are a number of options available to a business with separate departments when it is organising its administration:

- each department can be made responsible for its own administration
- the business can set up its own administration department
- the business can use other businesses to carry out some of its administration work – examples of this include cleaning and security services and the use of outside telephone call centres which will take telephoned enquiries and orders on behalf of the business

The diagrams on the next page illustrate these three possibilities.

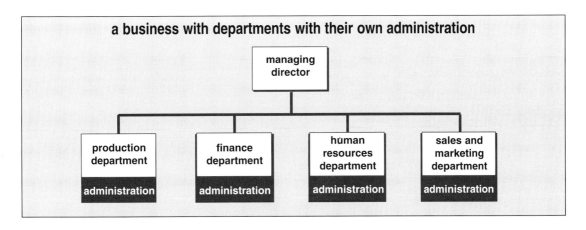

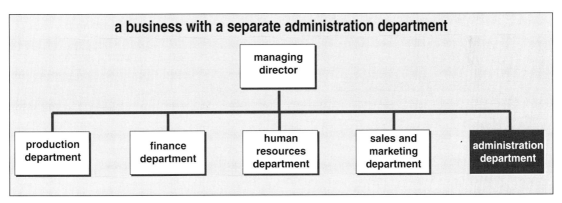

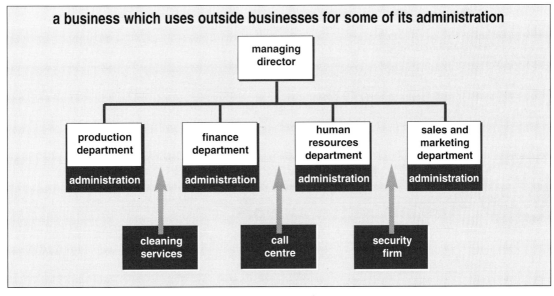

Now read the descriptions of jobs on the next page. They give an idea of what is involved in working in administration.

Jobs in administration

SARAH WHITEMAN

ADMINISTRATIVE ASSISTANT

"I work in the administration department on a part-time basis. I work with fifteen other assistants and a supervisor.

The work is certainly varied. I answer the phone, do word processing, filing and photocopying. We deal with all the paperwork involved with the running of the company, so we get to see what all the other departments are up to. I like working here, the atmosphere is good – the supervisor is strict, but has got a broad sense of humour!"

LEE CHEUNG

MAIL ROOM ASSISTANT

"I have worked in the mail room for three years now. We deal with all the incoming mail and packages, many of which have to be signed for. We open the mail, date stamp it and sort it into the various departments: anything to do with stock goes to production, cheques go to finance, job applications to human resources and so on. We have to make sure that the mail gets to the right person as quickly as possible.

We also deal with outgoing mail which involves collecting the post from the various departments, franking the letters and weighing any parcels. The afternoons can be very busy with all the deadlines to meet."

Activity 7.2

Administration at work

1   Talk to friends and family and make a list of all the administration jobs you can find out about.

2   Write a list of the administration tasks which can be carried out by outside businesses. What are the advantages of using people like these?

communicating in business

communication flow

Communication means getting a message across.

Businesses need to communicate on a very regular basis with people *outside* the business – with customers and suppliers, for example. They also need to communicate *internally*: departments need to pass information to each other, managers need to talk to supervisors, assistants need to complain to supervisors, and so on. As you will see from arrows on the diagram below, the communications flow in many directions:

- in and out of the business
- vertically – between the different levels of authority
- horizontally – between departments or functions

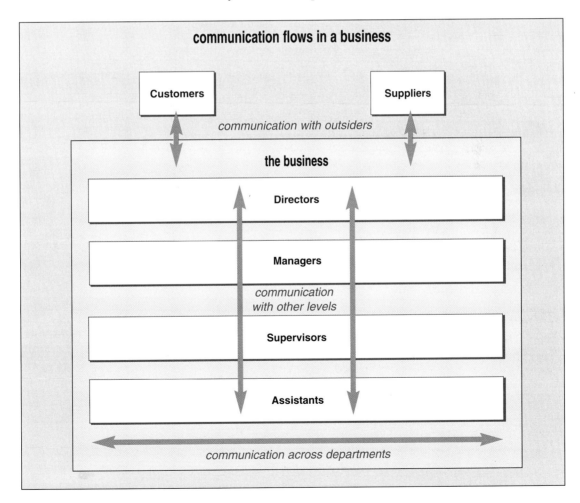

It is important to appreciate the different types of communication and see how they are used for different circumstances. When reading through the types of communication explained on the next few pages, put yourself in the place of a person working in business and think about the following points:

1 How appropriate is the means of communication for the person you are dealing with?

2 Should the message be kept private?

3 Will the message get to the person in time?

4 Should the content of the message be kept for future reference?

oral communications

Oral (word of mouth) communications include:

- meeting someone face-to-face and talking to them informally, eg serving a customer in a shop
- having a formal interview, eg when applying for a job
- talking to someone on the telephone, eg answering a customer enquiry
- leaving someone a message on voicemail (answerphone)

Activity 7.3

Communication
oral communication

You are working in business. What form of oral communication would you use in the following situations, and why? Choose from:

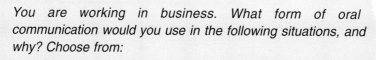

telephoning   **informal meeting**   **formal interview**

1   *You have the following message on your voicemail from a customer "Hello. This is James Brand calling at 2.00pm on 01908 675245. Please can you let me have the prices of the new range of copiers as soon as possible?"*

2   *You have arranged to speak to the Human Resources manager about a possible promotion.*

3   *You are told by the receptionist that one of your customers has called unexpectedly and is waiting in the reception area.*

written communications – the letter

the letter – house style

If you work in a business or receive letters from a business, you will note that the appearance and format of each letter is in a uniform 'house' style, a style by which that organisation is known. The most common way of setting out a letter is in the style explained on the next two pages. The example letter has been prepared by a firm of double glazing contractors, Wyvern Double Glazing. A customer, Mr J Sutton, has enquired about the installation of windows for a new extension.

elements of the letter

printed letterhead

This is pre-printed, and must have up-to-date telephone numbers and e-mail.

reference

The reference on the letter illustrated - DH/SB/69 - is a standard format

- DH (Derek Hunt), the writer

- SB (Sally Burgess), the person who keyed the letter in

- 69, the number of the file where Mr Sutton's correspondence is kept

If you need to quote the reference of a letter to which you are replying, the references will be quoted as follows: Your ref. TR/FG/45 Our ref. DH/SB/69

date

The date is shown in date (number), month (word), year (number) order.

recipient

The name and address of the person to whom the letter is sent. This section of the letter may be displayed in the window of a window envelope, so it is essential that it is accurate

salutation

'Dear Sir. . . Dear Madam' if you know the person's name and title (eg Mr, Mrs, Ms), use it, but check that it is spelt or applied correctly – a misspelt name or an incorrect title will ruin an otherwise competent letter.

If you are dealing with another business and are not sure whether the person you are writing to is male or female (you may just have an initial and surname in your records) you can always ring the switchboard of the business and find out. The same applies if the person is female and you are not sure whether to write to them as 'Mrs', 'Miss' or 'Ms'.

heading

The heading sets out the subject matter of the letter – it will concentrate the reader's mind.

body

The body of the letter is the main text of the letter. It must be:

- laid out in short precise paragraphs and short clear sentences

- start with a point of reference (eg thanking for a letter)

- set out the message in a logical sequence

- avoid jargon and slang expressions

- finish with a clear indication of the next step to be taken (eg please telephone, please arrange appointment, please buy our products, please pay our invoice)

Note that the body of the letter is the only part which has punctuation!

complimentary close

The complimentary close (signing off phrase) must be consistent with the salutation:

'Dear Sir/Dear Madam' followed by 'Yours faithfully'

'Dear Mr Sutton/Dear Ms Jones' followed by 'Yours sincerely'

name and job title

It is essential for the reader to know the name of the person who sent the letter, and that person's job title, because a reply will need to be addressed to a specific person.

enclosures

If there are enclosures with the letter, the abbreviation 'enc' or 'encl' is used.

Activity 7.4

Letters

1   Collect examples of letterheads from different businesses. A good source of letterheads is the junk mail that comes through the post and often ends up in the bin.

2   Design your own letterhead (on a word processing or desk-top publishing file) for an imaginary business you are setting up. Remember all the details such as telephone number and e-mail address that you will need. If you are feeling artistic, design your own logo for the business.

elements of the letter

Wyvern Double Glazing Contractors
107 High Street
Mereford
MR1 9SZ
Tel 01605 675365 Fax 01605 765576

reference ⟶ Ref DH/SB/69

date ⟶ 14 December 2000

name and
address of ⟶ Mr J D Sutton
recipient
23 Windermere Close
Crofters Green
Mereford MR6 7ER

salutation ⟶ Dear Mr Sutton

heading ⟶ Double Glazing of 23 Windermere Close

Thank you for your letter of enquiry dated 11 December.

body of
the letter ⟶ We are pleased to enclose a brochure with details of our double
glazing units, all of which comply with the most up-to-date building
regulations.

We will be happy to give you a quotation for glazing your new
extension. In order to do this we will need to send our surveyor to
measure up your property. We shall be grateful if you will kindly
telephone us to arrange a visit at a convenient time.

We look forward to hearing from you.

complimentary
close ⟶ Yours sincerely

signature ⟶ *D M Hunt*

name and job
title ⟶ Derek Hunt
Sales Manager

enclosures ⟶ enc

the memorandum

The memorandum (memoranda if you are referring to more than one) is a formal written note used for internal communication within an organisation. It may be word-processed or handwritten, and will often be produced in a number of copies which can be circulated as necessary. It can be used for situations such as:

- giving instructions
- requesting information
- making suggestions
- recording of opinions

A memorandum is normally pre-printed by the organisation with all the headings in place, and can be half page or full page in size. A completed memorandum is illustrated and explained below.

MEMORANDUM

To	K Roach, Finance Manager
From	Tim Blake, Sales Manager **Ref** KR/AC/1098
Copies to	Departmental Managers **Date** 23 June 2000
Subject	Product A163 Launch SuperSucker cleaner

Please attend a presentation of our new A163 SuperSucker cleaner on 24 July in the Ground Floor Conference Room. Details of the new product are attached and a fully working example will be demonstrated on the 24th.

enc

---

elements of the memorandum

Most of the headings on the pre-printed memorandum form are self-explanatory, as they are also to be found on business letters. As the memorandum is an internal document it does not need the name or address of the business.

'to' and 'from'
The name and job title of the sender and the recipient are entered in full, and so the salutation 'Dear......' and 'Yours ....' are not necessary.

copies to

Memoranda are frequently sent (as in the example above) to a large number of people; the recipients will be indicated in this section of the document.

reference and date

As in a business letter the reference indicates the writer, inputter, and file number and the date order is day (number), month (word), year (number).

subject and text

The subject matter of the memorandum and the text must be clear and concise.

signature

A memorandum can be signed, initialled, or even – as is often the case – left blank.

enclosures

If material is circulated with the memorandum, the abbreviation 'enc' or 'encl' should be used.

You should note that a memorandum can also be sent electronically as a message on an intranet (internal computer network) – a practice that is becoming increasingly common.

the message

There is no set format for a written message, which often results from a telephone call. It can be a scribbled note on rough paper, or it can be on a printed form. A typical pre-printed telephone message form is shown below.

TELEPHONE MESSAGE

for ....

date ....*time*....................

caller's name..

caller's organisation......................................

telephone no...

call taken by ....

message

notices

Businesses will also use notices as part of their day-to-day work. Examples of notices include:

- warnings – 'Wet Floor!'
- requests – 'Please turn this photocopier off when not in use.'
- staff noticeboard items – 'Staff Balti Night Out'

For a notice to be successful as a communication, it must be eye-catching, clear and accurate. It must contain all the necessary information – it must get the message across.

Activity 7.5

Communication
written communication

You are working in business. What form of written communication would you use in the following situations, and why? In each case draft out and then print out a suitable text on a word processing package. Make up names, dates and other details where they are not supplied.

1 Look at the letter from Wyvern Double Glazing Contractors on page 111. The surveyor has called and measured up the extension. Your estimating department has passed you a memo with drawings stating that the cost will be £4,500 plus VAT. You are to draft a communication in Derek Hunt's name to the customer setting out the cost and enclosing the drawings.

2 You are the manager of the Administration Department of a large company and have organised a staff night out on a riverboat for July 4, departing 8.00 pm from the South Quay, returning 11.30pm. The cost per head will be £9.50. Partners of staff will also be welcome (same cost). You need to let the departmental managers know these details and find out from them the number of people from their departments who will be coming.

3 You take a telephone call for your supervisor, who is at a meeting. His garage has telephoned to say that his car has been serviced and will be ready for collection at 4.00pm.

4 You are the supervisor of a number of staff who carry out data input in an office equipped with PCs. You notice that staff are placing mugs of hot coffee on top of the workstations, a highly dangerous practice, as coffee spilt in a computer could ruin it. You want to stop this practice by putting a notice on the notice board.

electronic communication

The growth of information and communication technology (ICT) has resulted in a revolution in the way communication takes place between businesses and also inside businesses.

intranets and e-mail

Many businesses are now linked internally by an **intranet**. This is a network system whereby people working in a business are supplied with computer workstations which are linked together electronically. This means that they can all have access to information held on computer by the business, eg customer details, product details, diary systems. In addition to accessing all this data, they can send each other electronic messages. This is 'electronic mail', normally known as 'e-mail'. It can be very informal. You may find that your school or college has an intranet installed. An intranet will normally be linked up on-line to the **internet** (see below and next page), usually referred to as 'the net'. Note that *an intranet* and *the internet* are far from being the same thing!

the internet and e-mail

The internet, or 'net', is a rapidly expanding network of private, public, commercial and non-commercial computers linked via telephone lines by internet service providers (ISPs) who operate servers (computers) connecting their subscribers together. ISPs communicate with each other by telephone links, largely by satellite. Any person or business who is 'on the net' just has to dial up through the computer to be able to contact other internet users, anywhere in the world, by sending e-mail or by using 'messenger' services.

websites

More and more businesses are coming on-line and setting up websites, not only for promoting their products but also for selling their products 24 hours a day, worldwide. A website is a series of interlinking pages set up on a computer server provided by an internet service provider (ISP). It is a 'shop window' for the business, and so successful have websites become that some businesses, for example the on-line bookshop www.amazon.co.uk trade only from their website.

A website normally has a 'contact' page which enables any visitor to the site to e-mail the business. A business with a website therefore has to deal with incoming electronic messages from the site in addition to the normal sources of e-mail.

rpnelson@goblin.com,,quotation	**1**

```
        To: rpnelson@goblin.com
      From: www.ritabooks.co.uk
   Subject: quotation

Dear Mr Nelson
Thanks for your e-mail enquiry of 1 December.
The title 'Bonzai for Beginners' ISBN 0 9510650 72 is available at £17.95. You can obtain it from most
bookshops and also from our website on mail order www.ritabooks.co.uk

Regards
H Bach
Customer Services
```

example of an e-mail message

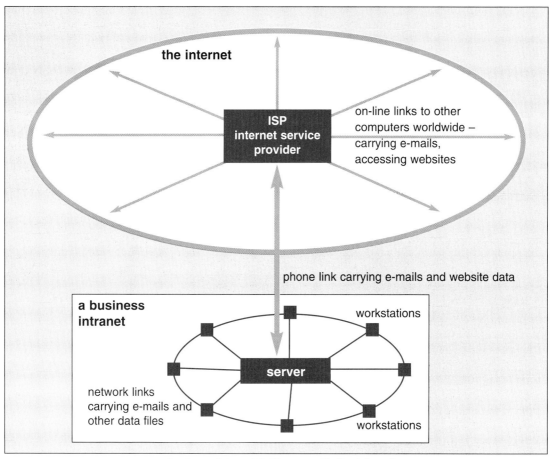

a business intranet linking up with the internet

fax

Another form of electronic communication is the fax (short for 'facsimile') which is a system whereby a sheet of paper is scanned by a machine in one location, transmitted down a telephone line and printed out by a similar machine at the other end. This is useful, for example, if you want to send a map, a price list or a drawing of a product to someone who wants it in a hurry. It is normal practice to send a fax with a 'fax header' which is piece of paper like a letterhead which sets out:

- the name and address of the organisation sending the fax
- the details of the person and organisation it is being sent to
- the date and the number of pages being sent

Faxes may also be generated on a computer file and sent direct down the telephone line from the computer. A typical fax header is shown below.

Osborne Electronics Limited

Unit 4 Everoak Estate, Bromyard Road
St Johns, Worcester WR2 5HN
tel 01905 748043 fax 01905 748911

facsimile transmission header

To: Jamie Milne, Buying Office, Zippo Computers

Fax number: 01350 525504

Number of pages including this header: 1   Date: 10 October 2000

message
Jamie
Just to let you know that the consignment you called about this morning was despatched last Thursday (5 October) and should be with you soon.
Regards
Jon Smart
Despatch Dept

---

videoconferencing

Videoconferencing involves an image generated by a camera on top of a computer being sent down the telephone line and displayed on a computer screen at the other end. This is useful for meetings where one or more of the people cannot be present. Modern technology is now making it possible for images generated by a small camera (webcam) to be sent over the internet.

videoconferencing in action

teleworking

Some businesses rely on electronic communications to such an extent that some employees work at home or in custom-built 'telecottages' in the country. 'Tele' means at a distance. They are usually linked on-line and communicate by telephone, fax and e-mail. They enjoy the advantages of a pleasant working environment and avoid the stresses and expense of travel.

work away from the city – a view of teleworking from BT

Activity 7.6

Communication
electronic communication

You are working in business. What form of electronic communication would you use in the situations below? Choose one of these for each situation:

e-mail   **logging onto a website**   **fax**

Explain in one sentence for each situation <u>why</u> you would choose that method of electronic communication.

1   *You receive a telephone call from a customer who is coming to visit your business tomorrow. He does not know where your premises are. It is too late to send him a letter and the road systems around you are so complicated that it will take you a long time to give directions.*

2   *You receive an e-mail from a potential customer in Australia. She wants delivery details of your products. Because of the time difference your office and the Australian office are never staffed at the same time.*

3   *One of your directors has to go to Paris for the day from London. The meeting is tomorrow. She wants to know very quickly if it is quicker and cheaper to get there by rail rather than by air. How could you find out from your office without having to contact a travel agent?*

the choice of communication

So far in this chapter we have looked at the different types of communication and the ways in which they are used, both when dealing with outsiders and also when dealing other departments in the business. Obviously, certain types of communication are used because that is 'the way things are normally done'. It is important, however, to appreciate *why* different types of communication are used in different situations:

- is it right for the person you are dealing with?

- should the message be kept private – is it confidential?

- will the message get to the person in time?

- is the communication needed for record keeping purposes?

On the next two pages are charts which highlight these points.

examples of communications used by departments in a business

a catalogue request and an order

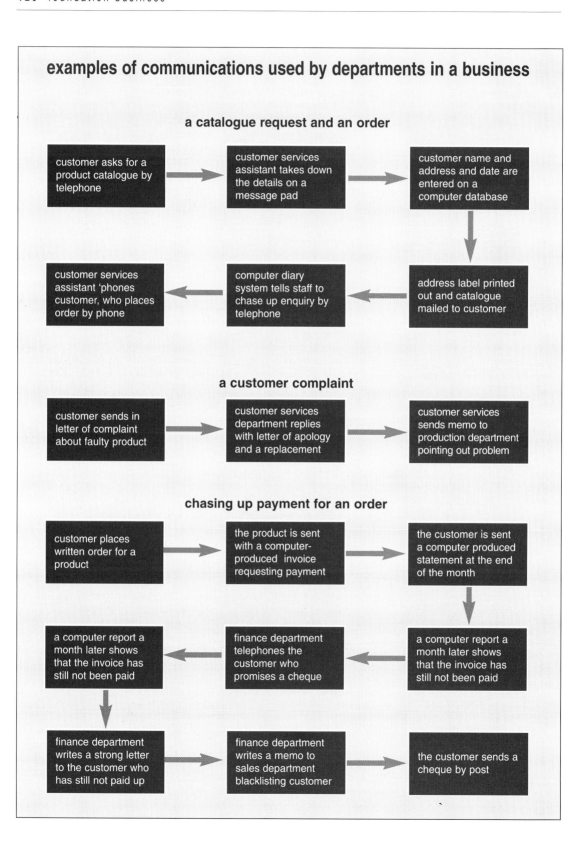

customer asks for a product catalogue by telephone

→ customer services assistant takes down the details on a message pad

→ customer name and address and date are entered on a computer database

↓

address label printed out and catalogue mailed to customer

← computer diary system tells staff to chase up enquiry by telephone

← customer services assistant 'phones customer, who places order by phone

a customer complaint

customer sends in letter of complaint about faulty product

→ customer services department replies with letter of apology and a replacement

→ customer services sends memo to production department pointing out problem

chasing up payment for an order

customer places written order for a product

→ the product is sent with a computer-produced invoice requesting payment

→ the customer is sent a computer produced statement at the end of the month

↓

a computer report a month later shows that the invoice has still not been paid

← finance department telephones the customer who promises a cheque

← a computer report a month later shows that the invoice has still not been paid

↓

finance department writes a strong letter to the customer who has still not paid up

→ finance department writes a memo to sales department blacklisting customer

→ the customer sends a cheque by post

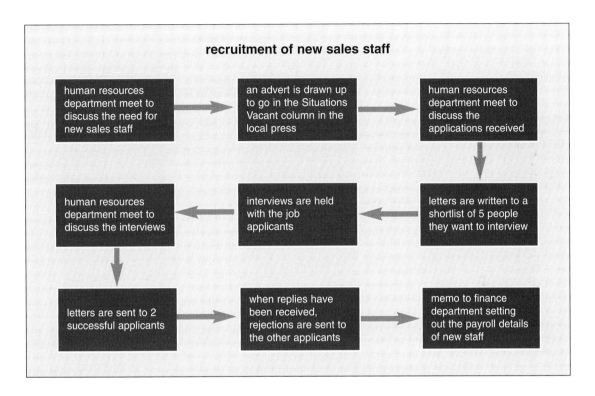

recruitment of new sales staff

human resources department meet to discuss the need for new sales staff → an advert is drawn up to go in the Situations Vacant column in the local press → human resources department meet to discuss the applications received

human resources department meet to discuss the interviews ← interviews are held with the job applicants ← letters are written to a shortlist of 5 people they want to interview

letters are sent to 2 successful applicants → when replies have been received, rejections are sent to the other applicants → memo to finance department setting out the payroll details of new staff

Activity 7.7

Communication
the right method?

Read through the flowcharts on these two pages.

1   *Give at least three examples from these situations of:*

   (a)   oral communication

   (b)   written communication

   (c)   communication using electronic means

2   *Which of the four situations requires*

   (a)   complete confidentiality

   (b)   a speedy response to the customer

3   *Give at least two examples from these situations of:*

   (a)   departments communicating with each other in connection with people outside the business

   (b)   the use of computers to help record the work of the departments

what have you learnt from this chapter?

- Administration provides the back-up needed by all businesses. It is a functional area which involves tasks such as:

  - dealing with the post and e-mail

  - keeping the records of the business

  - dealing with routine enquiries

  - setting up meetings

  - keeping the business premises clean and secure

- Administration can either be carried out by employees in each department or can be carried out by a special 'administration' department which looks after all the other departments' needs. Some businesses use outside firms for tasks such as cleaning, security and telephone answering.

- Communication involves getting a message across.

- Communications in business can be internal (within the business) or external (for example, dealing with customers and suppliers).

- There are a number of different ways of communicating:

  - by word of mouth – telephone conversations, meetings, interviews

  - in writing – memos, letters, messages, adverts, notices

  - using information technology, for example internal and external e-mail, the internet, fax, teleconferencing

- Good standards of communication are important. They help a business to work efficiently internally and to provide high quality service to its customers.

revision questions

For questions 1 - 4, choose one answer from A,B,C & D.

1   *Administration tasks in a business include:*

    A   *dealing with the mail, photocopying, cleaning the premises*

    B   *dealing with the mail, photocopying, market research*

    C   *photocopying, cleaning the premises, production*

    D   *cleaning the premises, security, quality control*

2   *Oral communications include:*

    A   *telephone calls, faxes, discussions*

    B   *discussions, interviews, e-mail*

    C   *interviews, discussions, telephone calls*

    D   *interviews, telephone calls, memoranda*

3   *The best communication method for sending detailed information to other departments within a business is:*

    A   *telephoning each department*

    B   *arranging a meeting for all staff*

    C   *writing a letter to each department*

    D   *writing a memorandum to each department*

4   *The best communication method for sending a technical diagram (a sketch drawn on paper) to another business is:*

    A   *e-mail*

    B   *video-conferencing*

    C   *fax*

    D   *teleworking*

5   *What is the difference between*

    (a)   *an intranet*

    (b)   *the internet*

8

Business costs, revenues and profits

Unit 3 Finance in business: investigating costs and revenues in a business, calculating profit or loss

what this chapter is about

All businesses have to pay costs when they start up for the first time and also when they are carrying on their day-to-day activities. Costs have to be paid out of the money received – the 'revenue' – of a business.

what you will learn from this chapter

- *Money coming in from the sale of the products of a business – the revenue – can come from the sale of manufactured goods or from the sale of a service.*

- *A business starting up for the first time or carrying on day-to-day trading will need to plan out what costs it needs to pay, eg premises, machinery, staff, advertising, rent.*

- *Some costs are one-off 'start-up' costs, eg premises, machinery.*

- *Some costs are day-to-day 'running' costs, eg wages, advertising, rent.*

- *Different types of business will have different types of costs, eg a clothes factory (manufacturing), a supermarket (retailing), a travel agent (service).*

- *A business makes a profit when the money received from its sales (revenue) is greater than its day-to-day costs.*

- *A business makes a loss when the money received irom its sales (revenue) is less than its day-to-day costs.*

- *A computer spreadsheet is a convenient and accurate way of calculating profit or loss.*

business revenue

Businesses raise their money from a number of different sources – the owners putting money in, banks making loans and the receipt of money received from the sale of the products of the business.

The amount of money received from the sale of the products – the sales 'revenue' – can often make the difference between the success or failure of the business. Revenue can be from the sale of:

- a product manufactured by the business
- a product bought in – as in the case of a shop
- a service such as a holiday, a taxi ride or a haircut

start-up costs for the new business

start-up costs

When a business starts up for the first time, or when it expands, the owner needs to plan what he or she will need to get going.

Start-up costs are 'one-off' costs you have to pay when you start a business.

There will be a number of 'one-off' costs involved. These can include:

premises

Premises could be a new factory (for a manufactured product), a shop or an office (for a service). You will probably point out that the owner of a business may not always have to buy premises – they can be rented, which is cheaper in the short term.

machinery and equipment

The business may need new machinery: production machinery (if it is a manufacturer), computers, photocopiers, delivery vans. Remember that these can also always be rented to save on start-up costs.

market research and advertising

Time and money can be spent in market research, finding out with questionnaires and interviews whether the new business idea will sell. People will need to be hired to do this, and this will cost money. Any new product will also need effective promotion and advertising, which can be expensive.

Activity 8.1

Ella MacPherson
start-up costs

Ella MacPherson has recently won some money on the Lottery and plans to set up a training business offering courses in office administration and computer skills. She has been working until now as a tutor at a local training college but is keen on being her own boss. She has drawn up a 'shopping list' of start-up costs:

Purchase of office premises	£95,000
Computer equipment and software	£22,500
Furniture and fittings	£9,500
Agency fee for market research	£2,500
Advertising in the local paper	£500
Advertising mailshot to local businesses	£2,000

1   What is the total of Ella's start-up costs?

2   Can you think of any other start-up costs that she might have to pay?

3   Ella has thought about buying some premises. Can you think of any alternatives to this which might save her money?

4   What other costs, other than start-up costs, might she have to pay?

running costs for the new business

In addition to the *start-up costs* we have just looked at there will be a wide variety of *running costs* that a new or an existing business will need to think about.

Running costs are day-to-day costs which a business has to pay.

It is important to know the difference between running costs and start-up costs. The difference applies to personal finance as well as business finance. For example, if you think about buying a new walkman, the start-up cost is the price of the machine, the running costs are items like batteries which you buy from time-to-time to keep it playing.

Running costs in business are normally estimated for the period of a year.

types of running cost

You will know from the unit 'How a Business Works' that there are a number of functions or departments in a business. There are running costs for each of these areas:

production

The cost of manufacturing a product or producing a service, eg sheet steel for a car manufacturer, goods bought by a shop to sell to its customers, air fares and hotel charges for a travel company, food for a restaurant, hair spray for a hairdresser.

sales and marketing

The cost of making sure that the right products reach the right customers in the best possible way: advertising, getting customer feedback, providing customer care.

human resources

The cost of employing staff, eg wages, recruitment costs, staff perks, training, Health & Safety (making sure people are safe at work).

finance

The financial cost of running the business: paying interest to the bank if money is borrowed, bank charges, paying accountants' fees.

administration

The day-to-day costs of running the business: insurance, rent, rates, power, stationery, telephone bills, postage.

Activity 8.2

Running costs for businesses

Look at the images on the next page to give you ideas and write down individually (or in groups), as many different running costs you can think of for

- *a services business*

- *a manufacturing business*

Use one sheet of paper for each business and the format shown on page 129.

You do not need to write down any figures at this stage, just the types of cost, for example wages and 'phone bills.

What differences, if any, can you see between the two types of business?

Activity 8.2 – use these images to suggest types of business running costs

description of business				
types of running cost				
production or service operation	sales and marketing	human resources	finance	administration

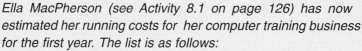

Ella MacPherson
running costs

Ella MacPherson (see Activity 8.1 on page 126) has now estimated her running costs for her computer training business for the first year. The list is as follows:

Training materials	£3,700
Advertising	£1,800
Staff wages	£28,000
Accountant's fees	£1,500
Bank charges	£400
Electricity bills	£450
Insurance	£1,800
Rates	£1,650
Telephone bills	£800
Stationery	£560

1 *What is the total of Ella's running costs?*

2 *Draw up a chart with six columns in the format shown on the next page. Use an A4 piece of paper turned on its side, or, if you can, set up a suitable computer spreadsheet. Make sure the left-hand column is about twice as wide as the other five. Head up the columns as shown.*

Using Ella's running cost figures shown above, enter the type of running expense (eg training materials, wages, bank charges etc) in the left-hand column and the money amounts on the same row in the column which best describes the type of expense (eg training materials = production cost of £3,700).

Add up each money column and write the totals on the bottom line.

*Add up the column totals and then check the total with your answer to **1** above. If the amounts are different you will need to check your workings.*

Ella MacPherson						
type of expense	production £	sales & marketing £	human resources £	finance £	administration £	
TOTAL						

Activity 8.4

Red Alert Limited

start-up costs and running costs

It is important to be able to tell the difference between start-up costs and running costs, because they will be dealt with differently in the accounts of the business.

Set out below are the figures for start-up costs and running costs of a new business that manufactures electronic security alarms. The figures are mixed up.

RED ALERT LIMITED – COSTS FOR THE FIRST YEAR

Electricity bills	£890
Premises purchased	£100,000
Office administration costs	£560
Equipment purchased	£45,600
Furniture purchased	£37,800
Rates	£2,190
Gas bills	£400
Insurance	£4,450
Wages	£120,000
Initial market research for business launch	£5,600
Electronic components used in production	£56,700
Cars and vans purchased	£55,650
Fuel and insurance for cars and vans	£7,400
Advertising during the year	£4,100

---

1 *Sort the costs into start-up costs and running costs. You can do this by drawing up separate columns for start-up costs and running costs.*

2 *Calculate the totals of start-up costs and running costs.*

3 *How much money will the business need in the first year to cover these expenses?*

costs in different types of business

Different types of business will have to pay different types of cost for the simple reason that they carry out very different types of activity.

manufacturing businesses

Businesses which make a product will need to invest in the resources for the manufacturing process.

Manufacturing start-up costs are likely to include factory or workshop premises, machinery and equipment.

Manufacturing running costs will involve wages of production workers, raw materials or components, the cost of running the factory as well as all the other normal business running costs such as office administration.

retail businesses

Retail businesses – eg supermarkets which buy and sell ready-made products – need resources to enable them to sell these products to the public.

Retail start-up costs are likely to include warehouses, shops, shop fittings, check-out equipment and delivery vehicles.

Retail running costs will include the stocks of the products that they sell, the cost of running shops, paying wages and all the other normal business running costs such as administration.

service industries

Service businesses such as travel agents and insurance companies provide a service and therefore do not need to invest in warehousing or to so great an extent in premises.

Service business start-up costs may be relatively low; they will need to invest in market research and also in the premises from which the business operates.

Service business running costs will include normal business running costs such as sales and office administration. The running cost of maintaining customer care will be important to service industries.

conclusion

As you will appreciate, no two businesses have identical costs. Generally speaking, it is more expensive and risky to set up a manufacturing business, but the rewards – in the form of profit – can be high.

Activity 8.5

Costs of different businesses

Set out below are the costs of three different businesses. They are a manufacturer of sports equipment, a shop and an employment bureau. Look carefully at the different types of cost and then carry out the tasks that follow.

expenses	Business 1	Business 2	Business 3
Factory premises	£2,200,000	-	-
Shop premises	-	-	£500,000
Office premises	£120,000	£150,000	£350,000
Vehicles	£67,000	£12,000	£155,000
Production line machinery	£145,600	-	-
Equipment	£6,000	£58,500	£176,500
Furniture	£37,800	£5,670	£67,000
Rates	£56,190	£1,870	£56,900
Electricity & gas	£5,400	£800	£23,000
Insurance	£24,450	£1,800	£56,000
Office administration	£8,560	£3,280	£98,000
Wages	£820,000	£86,000	£670,000
Raw materials	£556,700	-	-
Stocks of goods to be sold	-	-	£600,000
Advertising during the year	£4,100	£10,000	£120,000

1   *Decide which business is the manufacturer, the retailer and the service business. Write down your reasons for your decision.*

2   *Calculate the total cost of each type of business. You could use a computer spreadsheet set out in the format of the table shown above with an additional row for the totals. Remember to head up the columns with the type of business.*

3   *Discuss in class why the totals vary so much. How might this variation affect the type of business chosen by someone starting a business for the first time?*

what is profit?

a profit or a loss?

A business that sells a product or provides a service receives money from sales; it also incurs running costs. If the sales income is *greater* than the running costs, the difference between these two figures is the *profit* made by the business:

sales income less running costs = profit

For example:

sales income of £10,000 less running costs of £5,000 = £5,000 profit

What if the sales income is *less* than the running costs? The difference between these two figures is the *loss* made by the business. For example:

sales income of £10,000 less running costs of £11,000 = £1,000 loss.

It is common practice to show a loss in brackets, like this . . . (£1,000)

Activity 8.6

Calculating profit

Calculate the profit (or loss) made by the following businesses. If a loss has been made, show the figure in your answer in brackets.

	Sales income	Running costs
	£	£
Business 1	10,000	6,000
Business 2	12,000	8,000
Business 3	10,000	12,000
Business 4	15,600	7,800
Business 5	13,900	15,100
Business 6	145,000	89,000
Business 7	1,200,000	987,650
Business 8	235,000	270,000
Business 9	78,000	45,000
Business 10	12,560	9,654

the profit statement

At the end of a financial period – normally at the end of a year – a business will draw up a table of figures known as a *profit statement*. This financial statement sets out in a formal way the calculations you have been practising in this chapter:

SALES INCOME – RUNNING COSTS = PROFIT (OR LOSS)

A typical profit statement is shown below. The arrows and coloured text have been added to show what happens to the figures.

Study the profit statement shown below and then read the instructions for setting up a profit statement . . .

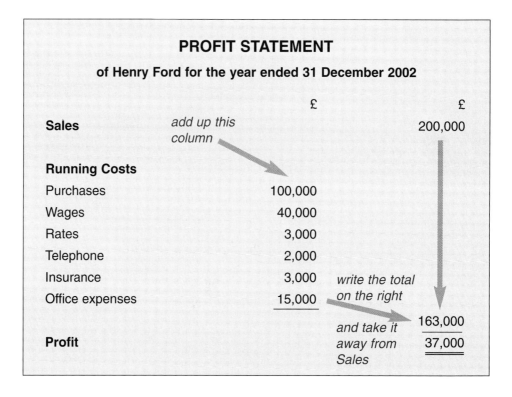

PROFIT STATEMENT

of Henry Ford for the year ended 31 December 2002

		£	£
Sales	*add up this column*		200,000
Running Costs			
Purchases		100,000	
Wages		40,000	
Rates		3,000	
Telephone		2,000	
Insurance		3,000	*write the total on the right*
Office expenses		15,000	
			163,000
Profit	*and take it away from Sales*		37,000

setting up the profit statement

1   headings

Write in the words 'Profit Statement' and then on the next line write the name of the business and the financial year the figures have been taken from.

2   set up the columns

You will need three columns:

1   one on the left for the words describing the figures, eg 'Sales', 'Running Costs', 'Profit'.

2   a money column in the middle for the Running Costs; this should have a £ sign at the top

3   a money column on the right with a £ sign at the top for the Sales and Profit calculation

3   Write in the Sales figure

The word 'Sales' goes at the top of the left-hand column and the amount (£200,000) goes at the top of the far right-hand column, under the £ sign. This is what the business has sold during the year.

4   Write in the Running Costs

The items which make up the running costs for the year are entered in the left-hand column and the amounts in the money column to the right of the words, under the £ sign. Draw a line under the bottom figure.

'Purchases' here means items bought which can be sold by the business, eg clothes for clothes shop or raw materials such as sheet steel and plastics used by car manufacturers.

5   Add up the Running Costs

Add up the Running Costs and write the total (it is £163,000) on the next line down in the right-hand money column. Draw a line under this total figure.

6   Work out the profit (or loss)

To work out the profit you have to take away the total of the Running Costs from the Sales . . .

£200,000 − £163,000 = £37,000

Write the word 'Profit' in the left-hand column and the Profit figure – here it is £37,000 – in the right-hand money column.

Draw a line under the Profit figure. You have finished! Now check your calculations.

If the figure at the bottom is negative, it is a loss. Show a loss in brackets like this . . .   (20,000).

profit statement on a spreadsheet

You will see from the format of the profit statement on page 136 that it can easily be set up on a computer spreadsheet.

Illustrated below is a sample spreadsheet file with the numbers filled in. You will see that you need three columns:

- a column on the left for the text, eg 'Sales'

- two columns for numbers (it is a good idea to leave some extra rows clear in the Running Costs section in case you need to input extra items of expense

Also illustrated at the bottom of the page are the spreadsheet formulas used for this spreadsheet. You may need to consult with your tutor or computer manual to check the format of the formulas used by your program. They may be slightly different from the ones shown here.

	A	B	C
1	PROFIT STATEMENT		
2	Name:		
3	Period:		
4			
5		£	£
6			
7	Sales		200000
8			
9	Less Running Costs		
10	Purchases	100000	
11	Wages	40000	
12	Rates	3000	
13	Telephone	2000	
14	Insurance	3000	
15	Office expenses	15000	
16			163000
17	Profit		37000
18			

	A	B	C
		£	£
			200000
13	Telephone		2000
14	Insurance		3000
15	Office expenses		15000
16			=SUM(B10..B15)
17	Profit		=C7-C16

Activity 8.7

Profit statements

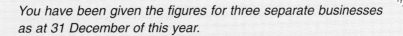

You have been given the figures for three separate businesses as at 31 December of this year.

You are to:

1   *Draw up profit statements for each of the three businesses on paper using the previous three pages as a guide.*

2   *Set up a suitable spreadsheet file (see the opposite page for guidance) and input the figures from your paper-based originals. Use the spreadsheet to check your original totals for accuracy.*

	Business 1	Business 2	Business 3
	Fairburn Foods	Grantley Supplies	Hardy Hi-Fi
	£	£	£
Sales	175,000	250,900	65,000
Purchases	95,000	102,984	45,000
Wages	45,600	67,800	15,600
Rent	5,000	5,690	2,000
Rates	3,450	4,010	2,100
Insurance	2,300	4,560	1,950
Advertising	2,000	13,450	560
Other expenses	200	2,057	500

what have you learnt from this chapter?

- *Money coming in from the sale of the products of a business is known as 'revenue'.*

  Revenue can come from the sale of manufactured goods or from the sale of a service.

- *A business, when it starts up, will have to pay costs which are one-off 'start-up' costs. These will be for items such as premises, computers and other equipment.*

- *Businesses also have to pay costs which are the day-to-day 'running' costs of different parts of the business, eg materials purchased, wages, advertising and rent.*

- *Different types of business will have different types of costs, eg a clothes factory (manufacturing), a supermarket (retailing), a travel agent (service).*

- *A business makes a profit when the money received from its sales (its revenue) is greater than its running costs:*

  SALES – RUNNING COSTS = PROFIT

  (where the sales figure is higher than running costs)

- *A business makes a loss when the money received irom its sales (revenue) is less than its running costs:*

  SALES – RUNNING COSTS = LOSS

  (where the sales figure is lower than running costs)

- *A business can calculate its profit or loss by drawing up a profit statement. This sets out the revenue and the running costs of the business over a time period, normally a year.*

- *The profit statement set up on a computer spreadsheet is a convenient and accurate way of calculating profit or loss.*

revision questions

Fill in the spaces in the text below below using these words:

start-up   **manufacturing**

services   **sales**

profit statement   **loss**

revenue   **running**

purchases

Another word for the the 'sales' made by a business is its ....

This money can come from the sale of goods or ....

There are two main types of costs which any business has to pay:

.... *costs and* ....

costs.

Different types of business have different types of cost. Businesses in the

.... *industry have to pay for* .... *of*

raw materials such as steel and plastics.

Businesses calculate their profit by means of a ....

.... *In this calculation, running expenses are*

deducted from .... *to produce a profit figure. If running*

expenses are higher than the money received by the business, a ....

has been made by the business.

9

Making and receiving payments

Unit 3: Finance in business:
Investigating methods of making and receiving payments

what this chapter is about

A business will need to make payment for its costs. It will also receive payments for the goods which it sells or for services which it provides. You will need to find out about the ways in which payments are made.

what you will learn from this chapter

There are four main ways in which payments can be made:

● *cash*

Business normally use cash for making payments for small items. They often operate a system known as 'petty cash' which is a cash 'float' used for making small purchases.

● *cheque*

Businesses often use cheques to make payments by post. They also receive cheques in payment for goods and services from the public and from other businesses.

● *debit card*

A debit card is a bank card which can be used instead of a cheque for making payments. It is often used by customers when shopping. It can also be used over the telephone or the internet to buy products.

● *credit card*

A credit card is a plastic card which enables you to buy something and pay for it later. Customers can use credit cards over the counter, over the telephone or on the internet. Businesses often use credit cards to pay for business running costs such as travel.

cash payments

who uses cash?

Despite the growth in the use of plastic cards, cash is the most common way of paying for goods and services – newspapers, magazines, sandwiches, cans of drink, bus fares, stationery – the list is very long.

Customers use cash when shopping and paying for services such as a hair cut and a bus fare.

Businesses use cash for making small purchases. A business will often keep a float of cash in a locked cash tin in the office for making small business purchases such as postage stamps, small items of stationery, office cleaning materials and so on. This is known as the **petty cash.** Page145 explains how the petty cash system works.

Businesses also use cash for paying wages, although nowadays more and more employees have their wages paid direct to their bank accounts.

the cost of paying by cash

Cash is easy for customers to use, but it can be expensive for businesses to handle:

- it has to be counted and checked by hand
- it has to be kept safe and secure in case of theft and it has to be insured
- in the case of cash wages it has to be collected from the bank

In fact, businesses would probably prefer not to deal in cash. They only do so because their customers insist on using it.

timescale

Cash is instant payment. The words 'cash payment' can sometimes mean 'payment straightaway'.

advantages and disadvantages of cash payments

advantages of cash payments	disadvantages of cash payments
payment is made straightaway	cash has to be checked by hand
ideal for small purchases	cash has to be locked up for security
cash is convenient to use	cash can be stolen

Activity 9.1

Making payments using cash

1   For what type of payments is cash normally used?

2   Why can cash be expensive for a business to look after?

3   State two advantages of using cash as a way of paying for goods.

4   State two disadvantages of using cash as a way of paying for goods.

discussion point
Do you think people and businesses will ever stop using cash?

receipts and petty cash

When someone makes a cash purchase for a business – for example going out to buy some stationery – it is important that they obtain a receipt. The person who does the accounts of the business will need it for their records.

When the purchase is made most cash tills show on the screen the money amount of the purchase and also the change to be given. The till will also issue a receipt for all purchases when cash, a cheque, a debit card or a credit card is used (see later in this chapter).

In the example below a customer has bought a pack of coloured paper and some computer disks from Everest Stationery.

A till receipt has been issued.

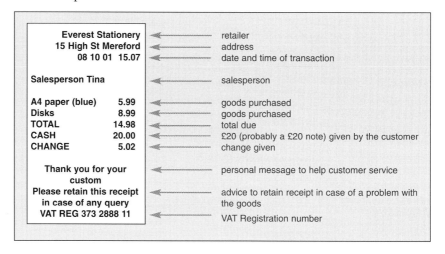

Everest Stationery	← retailer
15 High St Mereford	← address
08 10 01 15.07	← date and time of transaction
Salesperson Tina	← salesperson
A4 paper (blue) 5.99	← goods purchased
Disks 8.99	← goods purchased
TOTAL 14.98	← total due
CASH 20.00	← £20 (probably a £20 note) given by the customer
CHANGE 5.02	← change given
Thank you for your custom	← personal message to help customer service
Please retain this receipt in case of any query	← advice to retain receipt in case of a problem with the goods
VAT REG 373 2888 11	← VAT Registration number

a note on Value Added Tax (VAT)

You will see that the till receipt shown above quotes a VAT (Value Added Tax) registration number but no VAT amount. In the next chapter, VAT will be shown on a number of the financial documents you will be investigating and you will need to know what it is and how it works:

- VAT (Value Added Tax) is a government tax added onto the selling price charged for most goods and services

- the VAT rate is 17.5% (eg £17.50 is charged on an item costing £100)

- VAT is shown as a separate item on most financial documents **but not on receipts for purchases under £100**

- if you need to find out how much VAT there is in an amount on a receipt you should **multiply** the amount on the receipt by 17.5 and then **divide** the result by 117.5

  so . . . if the receipt is for £58.75, the VAT calculation is:

  £58.75 x 17.5 = £1028.125

  £1028.125 ÷ 117.5 = £8.75 VAT charged

cash payments and petty cash

Businesses often keep in a locked box a cash float known as the *petty cash* which is used to buy low-value items used by the business.

If someone working in the business needs to make a small purchase for the business – say some stationery needed urgently – they will go and buy it for cash and then bring back the receipt to the person in the business looking after the petty cash box. They can get the money they are owed by handing in the receipt and filling in a **petty cash voucher**. This business document records and authorises the transaction. Look at the illustration below – it shows the voucher used to reclaim the money for the receipt on the opposite page.

Remember that petty cash can only be paid out for business transactions – not for a takeaway you fancy at lunchtime!

PETTY CASH VOUCHER		No *800*
Date *8 October 2001*		
	£	p
A4 paper (blue)	5	99
Computer disks	8	99
	14	98
Signature *B Shaw* Authorised _____		

the total of what the goods cost

a description of the goods bought

the signature of the person who has bought the goods and is bringing the receipt

the person in charge of the petty cash box – the 'authorised' signature – will sign here

Activity 9.2

Receipts and petty cash

1   What is the VAT amount in receipts for £47 and £23.50?

2   Can a taxi fare to work be paid out of petty cash? If not, why not?

3   Obtain a supply of blank petty cash vouchers, either from your teacher or by setting one up with a computer drawing or publishing package. Use your own name, today's date and complete and sign vouchers for:

(a)   2 box files costing £4.70 each, including VAT

(b)   2 staplers costing £11.75 each, including VAT

payments by cheque

Cheques are commonly used in business by **customers** paying for goods and services either over the counter or by post.

Cheques are also used by **businesses** paying bills and other amounts owing. They are very useful for making business payments by post.

what is a cheque?

A cheque (see below) is an instruction by the person writing the cheque to their bank to pay someone a sum of money. Cheques are normally provided by the banks for their customers in books with counterfoils. When the cheque has been written out the details (amount, date and person being paid) are also recorded on the counterfoil and the cheque is torn out and given or sent to the person being paid.

tear off cheque here

| Date 5/11/00 | **Albion Bank PLC** | Date 5 November 2000 | 90 47 17 |

Pay
Marton
Computers
Limited

7 The Avenue
Broadfield BR1 2AJ

Pay   *Marton Computers Limited*

Two hundred and fifty pounds only   A/c payee only

£ 250.00 —

HARRIS N FORD

Harris N Ford

£ 250.00

083772   90 47 17   11719881

counterfoil   *cheque*

what happens to a cheque?

We will use as an example the cheque shown on the previous page. It is sent by Harris N Ford in payment for £250 owing to Marton Computers Limited for a computer printer which he has bought. What happens to the cheque? Look at the flowchart below:

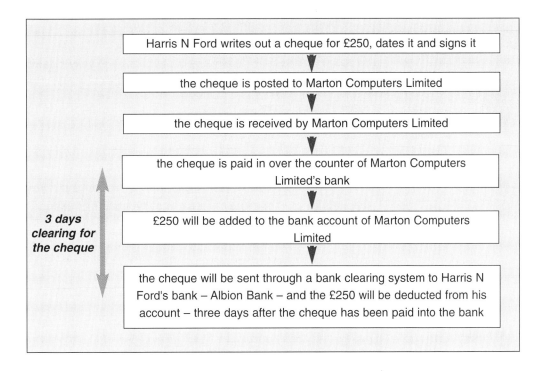

3 days clearing for the cheque

Harris N Ford writes out a cheque for £250, dates it and signs it

the cheque is posted to Marton Computers Limited

the cheque is received by Marton Computers Limited

the cheque is paid in over the counter of Marton Computers Limited's bank

£250 will be added to the bank account of Marton Computers Limited

the cheque will be sent through a bank clearing system to Harris N Ford's bank – Albion Bank – and the £250 will be deducted from his account – three days after the cheque has been paid into the bank

the cost of paying by cheque

Banks may charge for cheques written out and also when businesses pay in large numbers of cheques received from their customers. Cheques are otherwise cheaper to deal with than cash.

timescale

Cheques normally take three days to clear after they have been paid in. A business paying in a cheque for £100,000 received from its customer will have to wait three days before it can use that money.

problems with cheques

Cheques are more convenient than cash for larger payments, but things can go wrong . . .

bounced cheques

Sometimes a business will be given a cheque when the person writing out the cheque has no money on his/her bank account. What happens? The cheque will not be paid, it will 'bounce' back to the bank where it was paid in and the money will be taken off the account of the business that paid it in.

A bounced cheque is very bad news for the business which has paid it in – it basically means that it is not going to get its money!

errors on cheques

Sometimes an error on a cheque will mean that it will not be accepted by the banks. Errors can include missing signatures, the amount in words not being the same as the amount in figures, the name of the person being paid the money being wrong. Cheque errors are explained in more detail on the next page.

advantages and disadvantages of cheque payments

advantages of cheque payments	disadvantages of cheque payments
safer than cash	a cheque takes three days to clear
better for large amounts	a cheque is not guaranteed payment it can 'bounce'
cheaper than cash to operate	cheques with errors can be refused by the banks

Activity 9.3

Using cheques

1   Which is the better way of sending a payment by post – to send cash or to send a cheque?

2   What is the cheque counterfoil used for?

3   How long does it take for a cheque to clear when it has been paid in at the bank?

4   If you want your money quickly would you be better being paid in cash or by cheque?

5   If someone pays you by cheque are you as sure to get your money as if they had paid you using cash?

6   What is the cost to a business of using a cheque to make payment?

checking the cheque

When a business receives a cheque in payment, it must check that all details on the cheque are correct. If it does not 'check the cheque' it runs the risk of the cheque being returned by the customer's bank and the money being taken off its account.

Some shops will print all the cheque details (amount, date, name of shop) on the cheque at the till – all the customer has to do is to sign the cheque. This will obviously avoid mistakes.

details to check

signature	The cheque must be signed by the customer – it is completely invalid if it is not.
name of business	The name of the business receiving the cheque must be written after the word 'pay' and must be spelt correctly.
the date	The date must be written in the proper place at the top of the cheque. A cheque more than six months old is invalid and cannot be paid in.
words and figures	The amount in words and the amount in figures must agree – for example 'fifty pounds' and '£50' – if there is a difference, the cheque may not be accepted by the banks.
bank card	If the customer is using a plastic bank card to guarantee the cheque, the signature on the card should tally with the signature on the cheque

what to do if there is a mistake on the cheque

If a business is taking a cheque over the counter and the customer is still there, the mistake should be corrected and signed or initialled by the customer.

If the customer is not there – for example if the cheque had been posted, or if the customer has gone – the cheque should be returned to the customer with a polite request for the mistake to be put right and signed or initialled.

Activity 9.4

Checking cheques

Look carefully at the two cheques shown below and then on a separate piece of paper:

- *explain what (if anything) is wrong with them*
- *state what you would do to solve the problem if you were working for Sabre Stationery*

R Hanif is paying Sabre Stationery for goods costing £15.50. The date is 15 January 2001. The customer is still in the shop.

Western Bank PLC   Date *15 January 2001*   80 47 17

9 The Avenue
Broadfield BR1 2AJ

Pay   *Sabre Stationery* ——————————————————

Fifteen pounds only —————— A/c payee only ——————   **£**   *15.50*

R HANIF

123238   80 47 17   45195234

Helen Smith has posted a cheque to Sabre Stationery for supplies costing £200.50. The date is 15 January 2001.

Western Bank PLC   Date *10 January 2001*   90 47 17

7 The Avenue
Broadfield BR1 2AJ

Pay   *Severn Stationery* ——————————————————

Two hundred pounds 50p —————— A/c payee only ——————   **£**   *200.50*

H SMITH

Helen Smith

612349   90 47 17   11908236

---

payments by debit card

what is a debit card?

A debit card – shown below – is a plastic card issued by a bank to its customer which enables him or her to make payment for goods and services over the counter or over the telephone, without having to write out a cheque. Common examples of debit cards include 'Switch' and 'Connect' cards.

how does a debit card work?

We will use as an example a customer wanting to buy clothes costing £39.95 from a shop:

- the customer hands over the debit card and the goods at the till
- the shop assistant examines the card and then 'swipes' it through an electronic machine which automatically prints out a voucher slip
- the customer signs the voucher slip
- £39.95 will be added to the bank account of the shop, normally electronically through the linked computers of the shop and the bank
- £39.95 will be taken off the customer's bank account, electronically through the linked computers of the shop and the banking system

Note that no cheque is issued – the whole transaction is carried out by an electronic link-up between the shop and the banks

mail order and e-commerce payments

Debit cards can also be used to make purchases by telephone or with mail order companies. They are also accepted on many on-line shopping sites on the internet. Instead of the customer signing a voucher slip, the mail-order business or on-line shop takes the number of the card and processes it through an electronic terminal or through a secure link on the internet. Some people do not like shopping like this because of the level of fraud – some criminals get hold of the card numbers and use them to pay for things!

the cost of paying by debit card

Customers of businesses who use them may have to pay bank charges each time they use the card, or the use of the card may be free – it all depends on the bank and the type of bank account.

Businesses who accept the cards have to pay a small charge, 30p for example, each time they accept a debit card payment. They may also have to rent the till or terminal which processes the payment.

timescale

It takes three working days for a payment to get to the bank account of the business accepting the payment. If a customer pays for goods on Monday, the business gets the money on its account on Wednesday.

security of payment

A debit card payment is secure – it will not 'bounce' as a cheque might. Once the payment has gone through the till or terminal the business is sure of getting its money. There is, however, the danger of fraud (see page 151).

advantages and disadvantages of debit cards

advantages of debit cards	disadvantages of debit cards
guaranteed payment	it takes three days for the money to reach the business bank account
useful for mail order & e-commerce	the charge for the card and the till or terminal that the business uses
cheaper than cash to operate	the danger of fraud through criminals getting hold of the card numbers and making on-line and telephone purchases

Activity 9.5

Making payments using debit cards

1   *State two reasons why a business which sells goods might prefer a debit card payment rather than a cheque.*

2   *What are the costs to a business of accepting debit card payments?*

3   *How long does it take for a debit card payment get to the bank account of the business accepting payment after it has been processed by the terminal?*

payments by credit card

what is a credit card?

A credit card – shown below – is a plastic card issued by a credit card company. Common examples of credit cards include Mastercard and Visa. Issuers of cards include banks, building societies, shops, car manufacturers.

Credit cards are a means of payment used by customers who want to buy goods and services over the counter, by mail, by telephone, or over the internet and *pay for them later*. They are also used by employees of businesses to pay for business expenses, eg travel and hotel bills.

how does a credit card work?

A customer wants to buy a personal stereo costing £69.95 from a branch of an electrical chain-store such as Dixons.

- the customer hands over the credit card at the till
- the shop assistant will examine the card and then 'swipe' it through an electronic machine which will then automatically print out a voucher slip
- the customer then signs the voucher slip and takes the goods and a separate till receipt
- £69.95 will be added to the bank account of the shop, normally electronically through the linked computers of the shop and the bank

how is it different from a debit card?

- the customer does not pay straightaway
- the customer will receive a statement from the credit card company listing the £69.95 item together with other items bought on the card; the customer will be asked for payment within a few weeks

- the customer will make payment to the credit card company, normally by cheque, and often over a month after the purchase is made
- the payment can either be the full amount owing or a lower amount if the customer wants to pay the rest later

e-commerce and mail order shopping

Credit cards, like debit cards, may be accepted as a means of payment over the telephone, by mail order firms and by on-line shops on the internet. As with debit cards, there is the danger of fraud. Criminals may get hold of the credit card numbers and use them to obtain goods and services.

the cost of paying by credit card

Customers of businesses who use credit cards normally have to pay

- an annual fee for using the card, £10 for example
- if the full amount owing is not settled by the date stated on the statement, interest will be charged on what is left owing

In other words, using a credit card is another way to borrow money. It can be an expensive way to borrow as the interest rate charged can be high.

Businesses that accept credit cards have to pay a percentage on the amount of the transaction, 2.5% for example. In this case, if a business sells goods for £100 it will have to pay £2.50 to the credit card company. It may also have to rent the till or terminal which processes the payment.

In short, credit cards are one of the more convenient means of making payment, but they can be one of the most expensive both for customer and business.

timescale

It takes three working days for a credit card payment to get to the bank account of the business accepting the payment. If a customer pays for goods on Friday, the business gets the money on its account on Tuesday – three *working* days later. The customer, on the other hand, has a substantial time advantage. He or she may be able to pay for the goods or services listed on the credit card statement up to 56 days after they were bought.

security of payment

A credit card payment is secure. Once the payment has gone through the till or terminal the business is sure of getting its money. There is, however, the danger of fraud which worries many credit card holders (see page 151).

advantages and disadvantages of credit cards

advantages of credit cards	**disadvantages of credit cards**
guaranteed payment	it takes three days for the money to reach the business bank account
useful for mail order & e-commerce	the charge for the card and the till or terminal that the business uses
enables the card holder to borrow	an expensive form of borrowing for the card holder

Activity 9.6

Making payments
credit cards and a comparison
of methods of payment

1   What are the costs to a business of accepting credit card payments from customers?

2   What type of charges will a customer paying by credit card have to pay . . .

   (a) if the customer always pays the whole amount of the statement by the payment date set out on the statement?

   (b) if the customer only pays part of the statement amount by the payment date?

3   How long does it take for a credit card payment get to the bank account of the business accepting payment after it has been processed by the terminal?

4   Using a word processing program set up a table comparing the advantages and disadvantages to a business accepting different methods of payment. Use the format below if you wish and set it out as an A4 page. Make sure that you explain the advantages and disadvantages as fully as you can.

payment method	advantages	disadvantages
CASH		
CHEQUE		
DEBIT CARD		
CREDIT CARD		

what have you learnt from this chapter?

● *A business selling goods or services accepts payments from its customers. It also has to make payment for its costs.*

● *Cash is often used for making payments of small amounts. It can be expensive for the business to look after and to keep cash secure.*

● *The words 'cash payment' can also mean 'immediate payment'.*

● *Shops and other businesses issue receipts for cash purchases.*

● *Businesses often keep a cash 'float' available for making small purchases. This is known as 'petty cash'.*

● *A petty cash voucher is a document used by a business when it passes a petty cash payment through the system. It contains the details of the cash purchases and will be attached to the receipt.*

● *Cheques are useful for making payments through the post. They are also used by customers paying over the counter. Unless they are used with a bank guarantee card they have the disadvantage that they can 'bounce'.*

● *Debit cards are plastic cards which can be used for making payment over the counter, by telephone or over the internet. They can be used instead of cheques. For someone making a payment the money is taken off the bank account within three days. The business also receives the money in three days.*

● *Credit cards are plastic cards which can be used for making payment over the counter, by telephone or over the internet. The business receives the money in three working days, but the customer can pay later when a statement is sent. For the customer the credit card is a useful way of borrowing money when making purchases.*

revision questions

Choose one answer (A,B,C or D) from each of the following . . .

1   Cash is most suitable for making payments

    A   for small purchases

    B   through the post

    C   through the internet

    D   for large purchases

2   Which of the following cheques will not need altering?

    A   a cheque with no signature

    B   a cheque with a date five months old

    C   a cheque with a date seven months old

    D   a cheque with a date twelve months old

3   Business A banks at Albion Bank and gives a cheque for £50,000 to Business B which pays it an Barclays Bank. The cheque will clear and Business B will be able to use the money:

    A   on the same day

    B   three working days later

    C   five working days later

    D   when the statement has been received

4   A customer uses a debit card to make buy some CDs over the internet. Payment will be made:

    A   direct from the bank account of the customer

    B   by cheque from the bank account of the customer

    C   only when the CDs have been delivered

    D   by the date stated on the statement

5   The latest that payment for goods purchased using a credit card can be made is:

    A   on the day of purchase

    B   when the cheque clears

    C   by the payment date stated on the statement

    D   three working days later

10 Financial documents for buying and selling

Unit 3 Finance in business:
Investigating financial documents for buying and selling

what this chapter is about

When a business buys or sells goods and services it will deal with a variety of financial documents. The documents are completed by the buyer and seller and cover the processes of ordering the product, working out how much it costs, requesting payment and then making payment.

It is important that the documents are completed accurately – nobody wants the wrong product ordered, the wrong price charged or the wrong amount paid.

what you will learn from this chapter

- *A cash purchase is when payment for a purchase is made straightaway – as we saw in the last chapter.*

- *A credit purchase is when payment for a purchase is made later.*

- *A credit purchase will involve a series of financial documents.*

- *A purchase of a product on credit – when payment is made later – can be divided into three stages, each involving a 'flow' of documents (which will be explained in the text):*
  - *an order is completed by the buyer to order the product*
  - *the product is supplied and the seller tells the buyer how much is owed*
  - *payment is made by the buyer*

- *Financial documents must be completed accurately to avoid expensive mistakes being made.*

making a purchase on credit

financial documents for transactions 'on credit'

When a business buys goods or services *on credit* it orders the goods first and then pays later. During this process a number of different financial documents will be issued by the seller and the buyer. We will look in this chapter at a whole range of financial documents by means of a Case Study involving the purchase of fashion clothes.

You must bear in mind that not all purchases involve all the documents listed below. Many purchases are for services, eg office cleaning, and do not involve goods being sent. It is important for your studies, however, that

- you can recognise each of the documents
- you know what they are for
- you can complete a number of them

The financial documents shown here include:

- the *purchase order*, which the buyer sends to the seller
- the *delivery note,* which goes with the goods from the seller to the buyer
- the *invoice,* which lists the goods and tells the buyer what is owed
- the *credit note*, which is sent to the buyer if any refund is due
- the *statement,* sent by the seller to remind the buyer what is owed
- the *remittance advice*, sent by the buyer when the goods are paid for
- the *cheque,* which is completed by the buyer to pay for the goods

Note that a purchase on credit does not involve a receipt – this is normally only issued when a cash purchase is made (see page 144)

the flow of documents

Before you read the Case Study, examine the diagram set out on the next page. Down the columns representing the buyer and the seller are various activities which lead to transactions, which in turn generate documents.

As we have just seen, you should appreciate that not all the activities happen all the time – the order may be for services, the order may be placed by telephone, you may not get a delivery note, and a credit note is only used when an adjustment is needed.

Most of the time, however, things run smoothly and the invoice is paid following receipt of a statement.

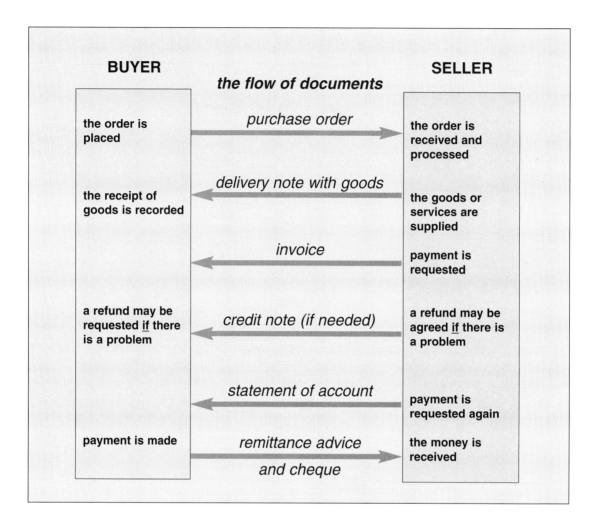

BUYER

SELLER

the flow of documents

the order is placed → *purchase order* → the order is received and processed

the receipt of goods is recorded ← *delivery note with goods* ← the goods or services are supplied

← *invoice* ← payment is requested

a refund may be requested <u>if</u> there is a problem ← *credit note (if needed)* ← a refund may be agreed <u>if</u> there is a problem

← *statement of account* ← payment is requested again

payment is made → *remittance advice and cheque* → the money is received

Cool Socks
buying on credit

Cool Socks Limited manufactures fashion socks in a variety of colours. It supplies a number of different customers, including Trends, a fashion store in Broadfield.

In this Case Study we see an order for 100 pairs of socks placed by Trends with Cool Socks. The socks are delivered, but some are found to be faulty, so a refund has to be made. Finally, payment has to be made for the socks.

The Case Study looks in detail at the purchase and sales documents involved.

now read on . . .

PURCHASE ORDER – *the buyer orders the goods*

purpose of the document	*to order goods or services*
who completes it?	*the buyer of the goods or services*
what happens to it?	*it is sent by the buyer to the seller*
why must it be accurate?	*if it is not completed accurately the wrong products may be ordered*

what happens in this case?
Trends orders some socks from Cool Socks. The buyer at Trends will post or fax the authorised purchase order shown below. The order will have been typed out in the office, or produced on a computer accounting program. The details of the socks will have been obtained from Cool Socks' catalogue, or possibly by means of a written or telephoned enquiry.

points to note:

- *each purchase order has a specific reference number – this is useful for filing and quoting on later documents such as invoices and statements*

- *the product code of the goods required is stated in the product code column – this is like the number you write on the slip when ordering something from an Argos store*

- *the quantity of the goods required is stated in the quantity column – socks are obviously supplied in pairs!*

- *the purchase order is signed and dated by the person in charge of purchasing – without this authorisation the supplier is unlikely to supply the goods (the order will probably be returned!)*

Trends
4 Friar Street
Broadfield
BR1 3RF
Tel 01908 761234 Fax 01908 761987
VAT REG GB 0745 8383 56

PURCHASE ORDER

Cool Socks Limited, Unit 45 Elgar Estate, Broadfield, BR7 4ER	purchase order no 47609 date 25 09 00

product code	quantity	description
45B	100 pairs	Blue Toebar socks

AUTHORISED   signature.....*D Signer*...date....*25/09/00*....

Practical exercises featuring the documents in this Case Study are to be found in the next chapter.

DELIVERY NOTE – *the goods are delivered*

purpose of the document   *it states what goods are being delivered*

who completes it?   *the seller of the goods*

what happens to it?   *it is sent by the seller to the buyer*

why must it be accurate?   *if the goods delivered do not tally with the description on the delivery note, the goods may be refused*

what happens in this case?

The delivery note is despatched with the goods when the order is ready. It is normally typed in the office or printed out by a computer accounting program. In this case, the delivery note travels with the socks, and a copy will be signed by Trends on receipt.

points to note:

- *the delivery note has a numerical reference, useful for filing and later reference if there is a query*

- *the delivery note quotes the purchase order number – this enables the buyer to 'tie up' the delivery with the original order*

- *the details of the goods supplied – the quantity and the description – will be checked against the goods themselves*

- *the delivery note will be signed and dated by the person receiving the goods*

——— DELIVERY NOTE ———
COOL SOCKS LIMITED

Unit 45 Elgar Estate, Broadfield, BR7 1ER
Tel 01908 765314 Fax 01908 765951
VAT REG GB 0745 4672 76

Trends 4 Friar Street Broadfield BR1 3RF	delivery note no	68873
	delivery method	Lynx Parcels
	your order	47609
	date	02 10 00

product code	quantity	description
45B	100 pairs	Blue Toebar socks

Received

signature......*V Williams*......name (capitals)...*V WILLIAMS*.....date..*5/10/00*......

INVOICE – *payment is requested by the seller (see next page)*

purpose of the document	*it tells the buyer how much is owed and when it has to be paid*
who completes it?	*the seller of the goods*
what happens to it?	*it is sent by the seller to the buyer, who checks it carefully and keeps it on file for reference*
why must it be accurate?	*a mistake could result in the wrong amount being paid; a wrong address could delay payment*

what happens in this case?

The invoice, like the delivery note, is prepared in the seller's office, and is either typed or produced on a computer printer using a computer accounting program. Invoices produced by different organisations will vary to some extent in terms of detail, but their basic layout will always be the same.

The invoice prepared by Cool Socks Ltd – illustrated on the next page – is typical of a modern typed or computer-printed document.

points to note:

addresses

The invoice shows the address:

* *of the seller/supplier of the goods – Cool Socks Limited*
* *the place where the invoice should be sent – to Trends*
* *where the goods are to be sent – it may not always be the same as the invoice address; for example a supermarket ordering a container load of bananas will ask them to be delivered to a distribution warehouse, not to the Accounts Department!*

references

There are a number of important references on the invoice:

* *the numerical reference of the invoice itself – 787923*
* *the account number allocated to Trends by the seller – 3993 – for use in the seller's computer accounting program*
* *the original reference number on the purchase order sent by Trends – 47609 – which will enable the shop to 'tie up' the invoice with the original order*

terms

The 'terms' are very important – they state when the invoice has to be paid.

Now look at the document and the explanations on the next two pages to find out what you have to check when you receive an invoice.

INVOICE – *payment is requested by the seller*

INVOICE

COOL SOCKS LIMITED

Unit 45 Elgar Estate, Broadfield, BR7 4ER
Tel 01908 765314 Fax 01908 765951
VAT REG GB 0745 4672 76

---

invoice to

Trends
4 Friar Street
Broadfield
BR1 3RF

invoice no   787923
account   3993
your reference   47609 ◄

date/tax point   02 10 00 ◄

---

product code	description	quantity	price	unit	total	discount %	net
45B	Blue Toebar socks	100	2.36	pair	236.00	0.00	236.00 ◄

GOODS TOTAL	236.00 ◄
VAT	41.30 ◄
TOTAL	277.30 ◄

terms
30 days

Practical exercises featuring the documents in this Case Study are to be found in the next chapter.

points to note and check on the invoice

You will need to check that the reference number quoted here ties up with your purchase order number.

The date here is normally the date on which the goods have been sent to you. It is known as the 'invoice date'. The date is important for calculating when the invoice is due to be paid. In this case the 'terms' (see the bottom left-hand corner of the invoice) are 30 days. This means the invoice is due to be paid within 30 days after the invoice date. The invoice date is 2 October, so it is due to be paid by 31 October.

The arithmetic and details in this line must be checked very carefully to make sure that you pay the correct amount for what you have ordered:

- **product code** – this is the catalogue number which appeared on the original purchase order and on the delivery note
- **description** – this must agree with the description on the purchase order
- **quantity** – this should agree with the quantity ordered
- **price** – this is the price of each unit shown in the next column
- **unit** is the way in which the unit is counted up and charged for, eg units (single items), pairs (as here), or 10s,100s and so on
- **total** is the unit price multiplied by the number of units
- **discount %** is the percentage allowance (known as trade discount) given to customers who regularly deal with the supplier, ie they receive a certain percentage (eg 10%) deducted from their bill
- **net** is the amount due to the seller after deduction of trade discount, and before VAT is added on

The Goods Total is the total of the column above it. It is the final amount due to the seller before VAT is added on.

Value Added Tax (VAT) is calculated and added on – here it is 17.5% of the Goods Total, ie £236.00 x $\frac{17.5}{100}$ = £41.30

The VAT is then added to the Goods Total to produce the actual amount owing:
£236.00 + £41.30 = £277.30

The 'terms; explain the conditions on which the goods are supplied. Here '30 days' mean that payment has to be made within 30 days of the invoice date.

CREDIT NOTE – *the seller gives a refund*

purpose of the document	A credit note is a 'refund' document which reduces the amount owed by the buyer. The format of a credit note is very similar to that of an invoice.
who completes it?	the seller of the goods
what happens to it?	it is sent by the seller to the buyer, who checks it carefully and keeps it on file with the invoice
why must it be accurate?	a mistake could result in the wrong amount eventually being paid

what happens in this case?

Trends has received 10 damaged pairs of socks. These will be sent back to Cool Socks with a 'returns note' and a request for credit – ie a reduction in the bill for the 10 faulty pairs. Cool Socks will have to issue the credit note for £27.73 shown below.

points to note:

* a credit note can be issued for faulty goods, missing goods, or goods which are not needed
* the credit note quotes the invoice number and states why the credit (refund) is being given

---

———— CREDIT NOTE ————
COOL SOCKS LIMITED

Unit 45 Elgar Estate, Broadfield, BR7 4ER
Tel 01908 765314 Fax 01908 765951
VAT REG GB 0745 4672 76

to

Trends	
4 Friar Street	
Broadfield	
BR1 3RF	

credit note no	12157
account	3993
your reference	47609
our invoice	787923
date/tax point	10 10 00

product code	description	quantity	price	unit	total	discount %	net
45B	Blue Toebar socks	10	2.36	pair	23.60	0.00	23.60

Reason for credit
10 pairs of socks received damaged
(Your returns note no. R/N 2384)

GOODS TOTAL	23.60
VAT	4.13
TOTAL	27.73

STATEMENT – *the seller requests payment*

purpose of the document	*a statement – which is normally issued at the end of every month – tells the buyer how much is owed*
who completes it?	*the seller of the goods*
what happens to it?	*it is sent by the seller to the buyer who checks it against the invoices and credit notes on file*
why must it be accurate?	*a mistake could result in the wrong amount being paid*

what happens in this case?

A seller will not normally expect a buyer to pay each individual invoice as soon as it is received. Instead, a statement of account showing what is owed is sent by the seller to the buyer at the end of the month. It shows:

* *invoices issued for goods supplied – the full amount due, including VAT*
* *refunds made on credit notes – including VAT*
* *payments received from the buyer (if any)*

The statement issued by Cool Socks to Trends for the period covering the sale (the invoice) and refund (the credit note) is shown below. Trends now has to pay the £249.57 owing.

STATEMENT OF ACCOUNT

COOL SOCKS LIMITED

Unit 45 Elgar Estate, Broadfield, BR7 4ER
Tel 01908 765314 Fax 01908 765951
VAT REG GB 0745 4672 76

TO

Trends
4 Friar Street
Broadfield
BR1 3RF

account   3993

date   31 10 00

date	details	debit £	credit £	balance £
02 10 00	Invoice 787923	277.30		277.30
10 10 00	Credit note 12157		27.73	249.57
			AMOUNT NOW DUE	249.57

Practical exercises featuring the documents in this Case Study are to be found in the next chapter.

REMITTANCE ADVICE – *the buyer sends a payment advice*

purpose of the document	*a remittance advice is a document sent by the buyer to the seller stating that payment is being made*
who completes it?	*the buyer*
what happens to it?	*it is sent by the buyer to the seller*
why must it be accurate?	*a mistake could result in the wrong amount being paid*

what happens in this case?

Trends have completed a remittance advice listing the invoice that is being paid and the credit note which is being deducted from the amount owing. Trends will make out a cheque for the total amount of the remittance advice. This is shown on the next page. It will be attached to the remittance advice and will be posted to Cool Socks in November.

points to note:

- *the remittance advice quotes the account number (3993) allocated to Trends by Cool Socks – this will help Cool Socks to update their records when the payment is received*

- *the documents are listed in the columns provided: 'your reference' describes the documents issued by Cool Socks and quotes their numbers; 'our reference' quotes the number of the Purchase Order originally issued by Trends*

- *the amounts of the invoice and the credit note are entered in the right-hand column – note that the credit note amount is negative, so it is shown in brackets; the total payment amount is shown in the box at the bottom of the form – this will be the amount of the cheque issued*

- *payment can alternatively be made by computer transfer between bank accounts (BACS); in this case a remittance advice is still sent, but no cheque*

- *a 'tear-off' printed remittance advice listing all the items is sometimes attached to the statement sent by the seller; all the buyer has to do is to tick the items being paid, and pay!*

TO   **REMITTANCE ADVICE**   FROM

Cool Socks Limited
Unit 45 Elgar Estate,
Broadfield, BR7 4ER

Trends

4 Friar Street
Broadfield
BR1 3RF

Tel 01908 761234 Fax 01908 761987
VAT REG GB 0745 8383 56

Account 3993   5 November 2000

date	your reference	our reference	payment amount
02 10 00	INVOICE 787923	47609	277.30
10 10 00	CREDIT NOTE 12157	47609	(27.73)
		CHEQUE TOTAL	249.57

CHEQUE – *the buyer sends a payment*

purpose of the document	*a payment document which, when completed, can be paid into a bank account; it enables people to settle debts, for example a buyer paying money to a seller*
who completes it?	*the person who owes the money signs the cheque and writes the amount in words and figures, the name of the person who is to receive the money (the payee) and the date*
what happens to it?	*it is passed or posted by the buyer to the seller*
why must it be accurate?	*if the amount is wrong the seller could end up being underpaid or overpaid; also, any mistake on the cheque could result in the banks refusing to let it through the clearing system*

what happens in this case?
Trends complete the details on the cheque – including the date, amount and signature – and send it to Cool Socks with the remittance advice.

points to note:
- *If a cheque is not completed correctly, it could be refused by the banks. Particular points to note are:*
  - *the cheque should be signed – it is completely invalid without a signature*
  - *the amount in words and figures must be the same*
  - *lines should be drawn after the name of the payee and the amount to prevent fraud*
  - *the current date should be written in – cheques become invalid after six months*

- *The lines across the cheque are known as the 'crossing'. The words 'a/c payee only' are an important security measure because they mean that the cheque can only be paid into the account of the person named on the 'pay' line of the cheque.*

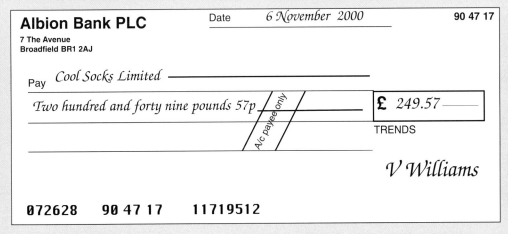

Practical exercises featuring the documents in this Case Study are to be found in the next chapter.

what to do with incorrect cheques

As we saw on the previous page, if you receive a cheque with a mistake, it may not be accepted by the bank you are paying it into. Alternatively it might be returned by the bank of the person paying the money because of a mistake, or because the person has not got any money in the account – it might 'bounce' (be returned by the bank), in which case you will not get your money. How do you avoid this situation?

correcting mistakes

If you receive a cheque with a mistake on it, you will need to get the mistake corrected and any correction initialled by the person writing out the cheque. If the person has posted the cheque to you this means in most cases posting the cheque back again with a covering letter asking for the mistake to be corrected. The most common mistakes that occur are:

mistake	what you do to correct it
there is no signature	send it back asking for a signature
the amount in words and figures differs	send it back asking for it to be corrected and the correction initialled
the name on the 'pay' line is wrong	send it back asking for it to be corrected and the correction initialled
the date is more than six months ago	send it back and ask for the date to be changed and the correction initialled
the date is missing	you can write it in! – this is the one situation where you do not have to send it back

Activity 10.1

Checking cheques

You work in the accounts department of Morton Components Limited. The cheques on the opposite page have been received in this morning's post. The date is 10 November 2000.

1   *Examine the cheques and write down what is wrong with them.*

2   *State in each case what you would do to put matters right.*

3   *Optional task:*
    Word process the text of a letter to be sent to the business which has written out <u>one</u> of the cheques.

(a)

| Albion Bank PLC | Date | 5 November 2000 | 90 47 17 |

7 The Avenue
Broadfield BR1 2AJ

Pay *Marton Computers Limited*

Two hundred and forty nine pounds 87p

A/c payee only

249.87

K J PLASTOW

K J Plastow

083772   90 47 17   11719881

(b)

| WESTSIDE BANK PLC | Date | 1 November 2000 | 78 37 17 |

22 Cornbury Street
Shelford SL1 2DC

Pay *Morton Components Limited*

One hundred and sixty five pounds only

A/c payee only

160.00

BACCHUS LIMITED

072628   78 37 17   23487611

(c)

| Britannia Bank PLC | Date | | 33 44 07 |

89 High Street
Broadfield BR1 8GH

Pay *Morton Components Limited*

Thirty five pounds 95p

A/c payee only

35.95

DAVIES MEDIA

H Purcell

987482   33 44 07   24221913

what have you learnt from this chapter?

● *A cash purchase is when someone buys something and payment is made straightaway; a receipt is normally issued for a cash purchase.*

● *A credit purchase is when payment for a purchase is made at a later date; a credit purchase normally involves the issue of a number of different financial documents which 'flow' in a set order.*

● *The 'flow' of documents involves:*

- *the buyer issuing a purchase order*

- *the seller sending an invoice and a delivery note with the goods, a credit note if any refund is due and a statement to advise the amount owing*

- *the buyer sending a cheque and a remittance advice to pay for the goods*

● *Make sure you can describe what the following documents do in the 'flow of documents':*

• *purchase order – the buyer places the order*

• *delivery note – describes the goods that are sent*

• *invoice – sets out what is owed by the buyer, and when*

• *credit note – allows a refund if there is any problem*

• *statement of account – sets out what is owed by the buyer*

• *remittance advice – goes with the cheque to the seller*

• *cheque – makes payment to the seller*

● *Financial documents must be completed accurately and checked on receipt to avoid the wrong goods being supplied or the wrong amount being charged.*

revision questions

Write the following words and phrases in the gaps in the text:

invoice   credit note   cheque   delivery note

purchase order   statement   remittance advice

We normally order goods using a ....

although sometimes we just telephone or e-mail an order. Then we get the

goods accompanied by a ....

Then we get the .... setting out how much we owe. If there

is anything wrong with the delivery such as damaged goods, the seller send us

a .... At the end of the month the

seller sends a .... which sets out all the invoices, credit

notes and payments. We normally pay in the week after this is received by

means of a .... We then send this off with a

.. .. which sets out the amount

being paid. Yes, checking is very important if silly mistakes are to be avoided.

It is the silly mistakes which cost the business money.

11 Financial documents – practical exercises

Unit 3 Finance in business:
Investigating financial documents for buying and selling

in-tray exercise

In this chapter you will practise completing and checking the financial documents explained in the last chapter. The documents used here are those used in a credit purchase – you order and buy now and pay later.

There are photocopiable documents in the Appendix on page 185. They are also available for download from the Osborne Books website: www.osbornebooks.co.uk in the Resources section.

To remind you of the 'flow' of documents that normally takes place, study the diagram shown below.

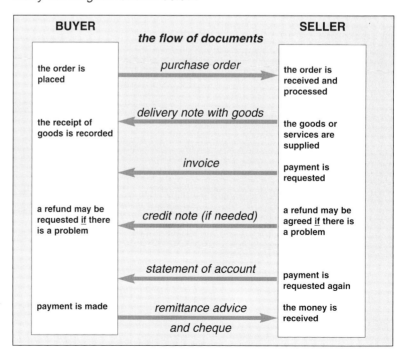

BUYER	the flow of documents	SELLER
the order is placed	*purchase order* →	the order is received and processed
the receipt of goods is recorded	← *delivery note with goods*	the goods or services are supplied
	← *invoice*	payment is requested
a refund may be requested <u>if</u> there is a problem	← *credit note (if needed)*	a refund may be agreed <u>if</u> there is a problem
	← *statement of account*	payment is requested again
payment is made	*remittance advice and cheque* →	the money is received

Activity 11.1

Buying goods

Blank financial documents are available at the end of this chapter and from the Resources section of the Osborne Books website: www.osbornebooks.co.uk

Work in pairs and play the roles of buyer and seller.

The buyer is a clothes shop Oasis, 5 High Street, Mereford MR1 3GF.

The seller is a clothes importer, Fashions Imports Limited, Unit 4 Beech Industrial Estate, Salebury, Manchester, M62 5FG.

You will need copies of blank purchase orders and invoices (see note above).

You should use today's date and the current VAT rate, but will need to make up the following details:

- *catalogue numbers*

- *order numbers and invoice numbers*

The buyer is to complete two separate purchase orders and the seller is to complete an invoice for each order. The orders are as follows:

(a)

> 100 pairs of tights (black) at £1.50 each
>
> 25 sweatshirts (green) at £8 each
>
> 50 T shirts (black) at £3.50 each

(b)

> 25 fleeces (red) at £15 each
>
> 30 pairs of jeans (black) at £17.50 each
>
> 50 pairs of tights (black) at £1.50 each

There is no trade discount available to the buyer. Add VAT at the current rate and round it down to the nearest pence.

Activity 11.2

Making a purchase with trade discount

Blank financial documents are available at the end of this chapter and from the Resources section of the Osborne Books website: www.osbornebooks.co.uk

You work for Deansway Trading Company, a wholesaler of office stationery. The company buys direct from the manufacturers of stationery and then sells to shops (but not to the public). Deansway Trading Company trades from The Modern Office, 79 Deansway, Stourminster SR1 2EJ.

A customer, Star Stationery of 126 The Crescent, Marshall Green, SR4 5TX, sends a purchase order to Deansway Trading Company:

Star Stationery

126 The Crescent
Marshall Green
SR4 5TX
Tel 01906 721354 Fax 01906 761912
VAT REG GB 0744 8383 56

PURCHASE ORDER

Deansway Trading Company The Modern Office 79 Deansway Stourminster SR1 2EJ	purchase order no 9516
	date (2 days ago)

product code	quantity	description
26537	50 boxes	Assorted rubbers @ 50p per box
72625	100	Notebooks @ 40p each
72698	250	Ringbinders (red) @ £2.50 each

AUTHORISED   signature......*R Eame*..date..(2 days ago)

A 5% trade discount is given to Star Stationery .

VAT is to be charged at the current rate on the total after the deduction of discount.

You are to *prepare invoice number 8234, under today's date, to be sent to Star Stationery.*

Activity 11.3

Checking invoices

task 1

A colleague in the Accounts Department of Cool Socks has prepared this sales invoice.

Check it and write down what is wrong with it.

You are then to draw up a new invoice with the same reference number and today's date. Assume the price quoted is correct.

INVOICE

COOL SOCKS LIMITED

Unit 45 Elgar Estate, Broadfield, BR7 4ER
Tel 01908 765314 Fax 01908 765951
VAT REG GB 0745 4672 76

invoice to

Oasis
5 High Street
Mereford
MR1 3GF

invoice no	876512
account	3461
your reference	87541

date/tax point

product code	description	quantity	price	unit	total	discount %	net
45R	Red Toebar socks	100	2.45	pair	254.00	10.00	279.40

GOODS TOTAL	279.40
VAT	48.89
TOTAL	230.51

terms: 30 days

task 2

You work in the Oasis clothes shop and have received this invoice in the post. You check it against the Purchase Order, the details of which are:

Order No 98372 for 50 pairs of dark blue Country trousers @ £12.45 a pair (code 234DB). You are normally given 10% trade discount.

The jeans were received, as ordered, on the same day as the invoice.

Check the invoice against the purchase order details.

If there are any problems write the text of an e-mail to The Jeans Company on paper or on a word processing file.

INVOICE

The Jeans Company

Unit 6 Parry Trading Estate, Southfield, SF1 5LR
Tel 01901 333391 Fax 01901 333462 email Jeansco@goblin.com
VAT REG GB 8762 54 27

invoice to		
Oasis 5 High Street Mereford MR1 3GF		

invoice no	942394
account	2141
your reference	98372
date/tax point	01 12 00

product code	description	quantity	price	unit	total	discount %	net
234B	Country trousers (black)	50	12.45	pair	622.50	5.00	591.38

GOODS TOTAL	591.38
VAT	103.49
TOTAL	694.87

terms: 30 days

Activity 11.4

A credit note is requested

An invoice for 50 reams of photocopy paper is shown below.

5 of the reams arrived damaged and Wintergreen Stationers have agreed to issue a credit note for this. (A ream is a packet of 500 sheets).

You are to complete a credit note for the damaged paper. Do not forget the discount and the VAT.

Blank financial documents are available at the end of this chapter and from the Resources section of the Osborne Books website: www.osbornebooks.co.uk

---

▬▬▬▬ INVOICE ▬▬▬▬
WINTERGREEN STATIONERS

75 Holmes Street, Broadfield, BR2 6TF
Tel 01908 342281 Fax 01908 342538 Email WGreen@newserve.com
VAT REG GB 0822 2422 75

invoice to		
	invoice no	9384
Uplands Insurance Brokers	account	3455
8 Friar Street	your reference	23423
Broadfield		
BR1 3RF		
	date/tax point	01 10 00

product code	description	quantity	price	unit	total	discount %	net
A4PPW	A4 photocopy paper white, 80gsm	50	1.70	ream	85.00	10.00	76.50

	GOODS TOTAL	76.50
	VAT	13.38
terms: 30 days	TOTAL	89.88

Activity 11.5

Sending statements

It is the end of the month of October in the Accounts Department of Wintergreen Stationers.

You have been asked to prepare the statements for two of your customers.

Their statements for last month (issued on 29 September) are illustrated on the next page.

These will be needed for the starting balance for October. The amount due at the end of September is the figure for Balance b/f at the beginning of October.

You will see how the starting balance (Balance b/f) is shown on the September statements.

The names of the customers and the transactions on the two accounts for October are shown below.

Tiny Toys Limited

Date	Transaction	Amount (£)
10 10 00	Payment received	105.00
13 10 00	Invoice 9410	560.00
20 10 00	Invoice 9488	3450.50
26 10 00	Credit note 12180	230.50

R Patel Associates

Date	Transaction	Amount (£)
10 10 00	Payment received	4999.83
16 10 00	Invoice 9433	1098.50
22 10 00	Invoice 9501	678.35
26 10 00	Credit note 12183	670.00

You will find a blank statement at the end of this chapter and in the Resources section of the Osborne Books website: www.osbornebooks.co.uk

─────────────────── **STATEMENT OF ACCOUNT** ───────────────────

WINTERGREEN STATIONERS

75 Holmes Street, Broadfield, BR2 6TF
Tel 01908 342281 Fax 01908 342538 Email WGreen@newserve.com
VAT REG GB 0822 2422 75

TO

Tiny Toys Limited
56 Broad Avenue
Brocknell
BK7 6CV

account   3001

date   29 09 00

date	details	debit £	credit £	balance £
01 09 00	Balance b/f			139.67
05 09 00	Payment received		139.67	nil
19 09 00	Invoice 9276	150.00		150.00
25 09 00	Credit note 12157		45.00	105.00

AMOUNT NOW DUE	105.00

─────────────────── **STATEMENT OF ACCOUNT** ───────────────────

WINTERGREEN STATIONERS

75 Holmes Street, Broadfield, BR2 6TF
Tel 01908 342281 Fax 01908 342538 Email WGreen@newserve.com
VAT REG GB 0822 2422 75

TO

R Patel Associates
78 Greenford Mansions
Mereford
MR3 8KJ

account   3067

date   29 09 00

date	details	debit £	credit £	balance £
01 09 00	Balance b/f			679.05
06 09 00	Payment received		679.05	nil
21 09 00	Invoice 9303	5345.50		5345.50
25 09 00	Credit note 12162		345.67	4999.83

AMOUNT NOW DUE	4999.83

Activity 11.6

Remittance advices and cheques

It is now the first week of November in the Accounts Department of Wintergreen Stationers.

The October statements from suppliers are arriving in the post. Two are shown on the next two pages.

You are asked to make out a remittance advice and a cheque (ready for signing) for each of them.

You are to settle both accounts in full.

Make up purchase order numbers for the 'our reference' column of the remittance advices.

A sample cheque is shown below.

Blank remittance advices and cheques can be found at the end of this chapter and on the Osborne website: www.osbornebooks.co.uk

---

Albion Bank PLC
7 The Avenue
Broadfield BR1 2AJ

Date _____

90 47 17

Pay _____

_____ A/c payee only

£ _____

WINTERGREEN STATIONERS

123238   90 47 17   45195234

statement 1

STATEMENT OF ACCOUNT
PRONTO SUPPLIES

Unit 17, Blakefield Estate, Broadfield, BR4 9TG
Tel 01908 482111 Fax 01908 482471 Email Pronto@imp.com
VAT REG GB4452 2411 21

TO

Wintergreen Stationers 75 Holmes Street Broadfield BK2 6TF	account	2343
	date	31 10 00

date	details	debit £	credit £	balance £
02 10 00	Balance b/f			234.75
05 10 00	Payment received		234.75	nil
19 10 00	Invoice 8717	290.75		290.75
22 10 00	Invoice 8734	654.10		944.85
25 10 00	Invoice 8766	125.00		1069.85

	AMOUNT NOW DUE	1069.85

statement 2

STATEMENT
HILLIARD & BROWN

99 Caxton Street, Norwich, NR2 7VB
Tel 01603 342281 Fax 01603 342538 Email Hillibrown@newserve.com
VAT REG GB 4532 1121 06

TO

Wintergreen Stationers
75 Holmes Street
Broadfield
BK2 6TF

account   2234

date   31 10 00

date	details	debit £	credit £	balance £
02 10 00	Balance b/f			560.00
05 10 00	Payment received		560.00	nil
19 10 00	Invoice 3213	1256.90		1256.90
22 10 00	Invoice 3244	987.60		2244.50
25 10 00	Credit note 4501		135.00	2109.50

AMOUNT NOW DUE	2109.50

Appendix – Financial documents

This appendix contains financial documents which you can photocopy for use in student activities.

The documents are:

1   purchase order

2   invoice

3   credit note

4   statement of account

5   remittance advice

6   cheque

The documents are also available in A4 format from www.osbornebooks.co.uk

PURCHASE ORDER

from

to

purchase order no

date

product code	quantity	description

AUTHORISED

signature...date..

INVOICE

from

to

invoice no

account

your reference

date/tax point

product code	description	quantity	price	unit	total	discount %	net

terms

GOODS TOTAL	
VAT	
TOTAL	

CREDIT NOTE

from

to

credit note no

account

your reference

our invoice

date/tax point

product code	description	quantity	price	unit	total	discount %	net

reasons for credit

GOODS TOTAL	
VAT	
TOTAL	

STATEMENT OF ACCOUNT

from

to

account

date

date	details	debit	credit	balance

	AMOUNT NOW DUE	

REMITTANCE ADVICE

to

from

account no

date

date	your reference	our reference	payment amount

CHEQUE TOTAL

Bank:

Date

Branch:

Pay

A/c payee only

index